"'To be a man, you've got to *see* a man.' In a fatherless generation where the picture of manhood is distorted and almost nonexistent, we have a generation of young men crying out for one thing—*definition*. By and large we don't know who we are, why we're here, where we're going, and most importantly who we are to become. With the heart of a father Patrick Morley gives my generation hope by painting a picture of what we are to become as young men looking in the mirror at the reflection of our own lives."

Jason Perry, member of PlusOne
Author, *You Are Not Your Own*

the young
man in the mirror

PATRICK MORLEY

the young man in the mirror

A RITE OF PASSAGE INTO MANHOOD

BROADMAN
&HOLMAN
PUBLISHERS

Nashville, Tennessee

0–8054–2641–8

Published by Broadman & Holman Publishers
Nashville, Tennessee

The author is represented by the literary agency of
Wolgemuth & Associates, Inc.

Dewey Decimal Classification: 305.31
Subject Heading: YOUNG MEN \ CHRISTIAN LIFE

4 5 6 7 8 9 10 07 06 05 04 03

To my son, John, and his new wife, Kristie.
Son, half the lessons in this book you learned from me.
The other half I learned from you.

contents

acknowledgments

My special thanks to fifteen young men who participated in a book planning session that determined the content of this book: Cameron Allen, Derrick Allen, J. T. Bachman, Hace Cargo, Mark Hammond, Greg Jackson, John Morley, Ian Pfingsten, Drew Reisinger, Ben Rupp, Nate Rupp, Cory Shaffer, Braden Wyatt, Spencer Wyatt, and Michael Yoast.

We used a technique called "storyboarding" that let everyone have an equal voice. Because of their input, the book you have in your hands is the most democratic writing I've ever undertaken.

Several youth workers provided direction and suggestions: Jeff Jakes, Del Wright, Brian Pikalow, Phil Newberry, and Chris Duggar. Thank you.

Once the book was written into a draft, Jeff Jakes, our youth pastor, helped me invite seven young men to be in a "field test" group. We met weekly and went through the book line by line. Their contributions to the final version are considerable, and I want to thank them especially: Cameron Allen, Hace Cargo, Collin Graff, David Popper, Braden Wyatt, Spencer Wyatt, and Michael Yoast. You guys are the best. Jeff Jakes also led a group, and I appreciate the special contributions of Charlie Kidd, Taylor Meier, and Brian Mauger. Thanks, guys.

Thanks to Len Goss, my sponsoring editor at Broadman & Holman Publishers; to John Landers, project editor; and to other B&H staffers who worked on the book, including Kim Overcash, Courtney Brooks, Paul Mikos, Greg Pope, David Woodard, and David Shepherd. You, too, Ken Stephens, for a long friendship. As always, I also appreciate the above and beyond contributions of my literary agent and dear friend, Robert Wolgemuth.

introduction

You are going to be a man. This, of course, is inevitable. The question is, will you be a good one or a bad one?

The purpose of this book is to initiate you into manhood. We will answer the questions, "What does it mean to be a man? How do you become one?" It is a book for young men in high school who want to do something with their lives. It is straight talk, not watered down and not hyped up.

I realize it is common today, even popular, to think that our existence is pointless, that traditional values are unfounded, and that there is no objective ground for truth.

One youth worker told me that he doesn't think you give a rip about purpose, the future, or doing something with your life. He thinks you are only interested in yourself. I respect his opinion, but I disagree. My own experiences with young men have been much more optimistic.

No man wants to be a shooting star that streaks across the sky one night, then disappears. You have been created for a purpose. A lot of what it means to become a man is to discover this purpose.

A man's most intense need is his desire to do something with his life—to be significant, to make his life count. We are created to make a difference, and a man cannot find happiness until he discovers the purpose for which he exists.

Most of my life has been spent trying to persuade men—many of them your father's age—to be more robust for Jesus Christ. I think it would be fair for you to ask, "Why isn't my parents' generation more sold out for Jesus Christ?"

Frankly, I can't explain it. Maybe it's materialism. Maybe we're just selfish. This I do know: Most men only know enough about God to be disappointed with him. Their faith is lukewarm, and their testimony should make them blush. We became, by and large, a generation of cultural Christians rather than biblical Christians.

That's beginning to change, but now your generation gets its shot at living radically for Jesus Christ. We'll see how it goes. The purpose of this book is to give you a head start.

You can read this book on your own or with a group of guys. Get a father, mentor, upperclassman, or youth pastor to lead discussion. There is a Discussion Leader's Guide at the end.

PART

1 | BECOMING A MAN

1 | you are not alone

I quit high school. I'm not proud of it and wouldn't mention it at all except that I want to make a point: I quit because I couldn't make "my world" work. It just didn't make any sense.

I didn't quit because I was a bum or a drug addict. I quit because I wanted to do something with my life, but everything felt like it was against me. I'm not saying it was, but just that it felt that way.

A voice inside my head was screaming, "You were created for a purpose!" Everything around me was screaming back, "What's the use? There's no point to any of it." Nothing made sense.

I just couldn't fit all the pieces together. I needed a plan for my life, but all I was getting were conflicting bits of a story that didn't make any sense.

- My science teacher told me the universe is made up of matter randomly arranged by chance.
- My biology teacher taught me that I evolved from a monkey.
- My English teacher thought that grammar was going to solve the problems of the world.
- My math teachers taught whatever it is they talk about in those classes.
- My church was vaguely trying to teach me the importance of religion (until we stopped going as a family when I was in high school).

> *I wanted my life to count, but nothing made sense.*

- My coaches taught me about teamwork and perseverance.
- My dad taught me about the value of hard work, keeping my word, and how to treat a lady.
- My mom taught me about the importance of family.

I'm not saying that I actually "learned" what they were teaching or that they were right, but this is what I was being taught. The problem was that nobody ever took all of these moral, spiritual, and academic lessons and tied them together into a *system, worldview,* or *story* that made any sense to me.

> My teachers taught me that I evolved from a monkey and that everything was chance.

And then there were my friends. Today I know that they were just as confused as I was, but we all tried to pretend we had it together. We taught each other a few things the adults failed to mention. We taught each other about sex, drinking, smoking, partying, friendship, cussing, shooting pool, having fun, and racing cars. We had fun and learned some things, but we also led each other astray.

So I began to flounder. School was boring. My part-time job was boring. My family was boring. I was boring. I was also angry and depressed. I couldn't get motivated. My temper flared up at almost any provocation, real or imagined. I was too immature to know that I was immature. I was putting my whole family through a living hell—even though at the time I did not know this, nor would I have cared if I had known. I was in pain.

My stomach was tied up in knots. I had no idea of who I was, why I existed, where I was going, or how to get there. Basically, I was an unhappy person.

> My friends and I led each other astray.

If I'm wrong about this next statement I apologize, but the adults in my life either didn't know how to help (rescue) me, or they didn't care. I don't mean to sound harsh. I'm not claiming that I was a victim. I'm not blaming anyone else for my decisions. I confess that I was a rebel.

But it's just not that easy to put a label on me. I was complex, and so are you. Yes, I was a rebel. But could I have been a better rebel—a rebel with a cause—if someone had seen potential in me, taken me under their wing, and mentored me? The answer for you and me is an emphatic, "Yes!"

The day after I quit high school my dad drove me down to the Army enlistment office. Wisely, he wasn't going to let me hang around the house. The next thing I remember was waking up at 5:00 A.M. to the screaming voice of a ferocious-looking drill sergeant who rolled me out of bed for a three-mile run in combat boots before breakfast.

> Could I have been shaped and molded into a rebel with a cause?

Dazed with confusion, I remember wondering, *What's going on here? What's this all about? How did I end up here?* I didn't have a clue.

Oddly, *the structure* of the Army actually *created a sense of safety* rather than confinement. My wings began to spread. Soon I had a chance to take a GED test for a high school equivalency diploma. Then I started taking classes at a branch campus that N.C. State University operated at Ft. Bragg, where I was stationed.

Today I know what happened to me and why. I'll be sharing some of those lessons in this book.

Q *Which one of the following words most caught your attention, and why? Quit, purpose, count, monkey, chance, confused, bored, angry, depressed, not motivated, temper astray, lonely, unhappy, rebel, a cause, no clue, structure, safety.*

Is There Something Wrong with You?

In this chapter I want you to see that you are not abnormal. Every guy you know is dealing with exactly the same feelings and issues as you are. The problem is that nobody wants anybody else to know it. But they are.

All the young men I know today are also struggling to make sense of their world—even the ones who seem (or pretend) to have their act together. Why is this?

Everything is changing. You haven't experienced a lot of these feelings and situations before now. You are unsure of yourself. No doubt your self-confidence has taken a beating from your peers (all the little jokes at your expense). You are filled with conflicting feelings, thoughts, and desires. Some of these are positive and some are negative.

> *You are not abnormal.*

Here's the bottom line: Until you were 12 years old your mind, body, and emotions were developing under one set of rules. When you hit puberty at 13, the rules changed. And now every year is going to be a totally different set of rules. You can expect a lot of emotional struggles. Every year you will experience body changes, mental growth, and mood swings until you have settled into an adult life.

Q *"You are not abnormal." Do you agree or not, and why? How does it make you feel to know that you are not abnormal?*

The Difficult Decade

Between the ages of 16 and 26 your life will change more dramatically and more often than during any other period of your life.

Dr. James Dobson, founder of Focus on the Family, calls this "the difficult decade." It will be difficult because of all the choices you will make—and what can happen if you make the wrong choices.

A Challenge

The next decade also will be one of the most exciting times of your life. By the time you reach twenty-six you will likely complete your education, choose a vocation, take a job, earn a regular paycheck, move into your own place, marry, start a family, join a church, have a personal ministry, volunteer somewhere in your community, vote, and pay taxes.

> *You can take a lot of the "difficult" out of the "decade."*

How will you know what to do? How will you make the right choices? How will you "do something with your life"?

You learn by becoming a contributing member of both your community and the kingdom of God right now, right here, right where you are. The Bible puts it like this: "Don't let anyone look down on you because you are young, but set an example for the believers in speech, in life, in love, in faith and in purity" (1 Timothy 4:12).

Q *"Between the ages of 16 and 26 your life will change more dramatically and more often than during any other period of your life." Does this sound right to you or not, and why?*

How badly do you want to do something with your life? How does that motivate you now?

What is the challenge?

2 | manhood: what does it mean to be a man?

Dear Dad,

I must be coming of age. I'm wondering more and more about questions like, "Who am I?" and "What is my life about?" Dad, I want to do something with my life.

A lot of my friends act like they don't take life seriously. I guess I try to act that way myself a lot of the time. But it isn't true—for them or me. In fact, we are all pretty much alike in that way. Of course, having fun is a top priority, but most kids I know have a serious side. We're just afraid of being ridiculed—it's a self-defense mechanism.

I know there are a lot of cynics running around. A lot of kids my age have bought into this whole thing about no meaning, no purpose, no absolutes, no real truth, no right or wrong, no direction, and anything goes. I can see their point, but I'd like more out of life than that kind of despair. In my heart, I suspect it's only because they really wish they could find some true meaning.

Sure, I'm a little afraid of the future, but mostly I'm filled with hopes and dreams about making a good life. As for me, I want to get a good education, find a good wife, have children of my own, get a good job, do meaningful work, be a good citizen, live an honest and moral life, have God in my life, be part of a strong church, and not lose my idealism. I want to make good

> *A lot of kids my age have bought into this whole thing about no meaning, no purpose, no absolutes, no real truth, no right or wrong, no direction, and anything goes.*

> *But I'd like more out of life than that kind of despair.*

choices. *I really do want my life to count. I want it to matter that I walked the face of the earth.*

So, first, I want to thank you for bringing me into the world. Although the world seems a little crazy at times, I am optimistic about finding my place and making a difference. Mom has done a good job to make me think this way—always stressing the importance of a good education and believing in myself. She thinks I could do anything which, of course, we both know isn't true. But it's nice she talks that way. She has worked really hard to keep us together as a family. I love and appreciate her for it.

Dad, I've got lots of questions about what it means to be a man—questions that only a man who's been there can answer. I'm talking about things a mom— even a great mom—just can't know. Some things just seem like "men only" issues. Here are some of the things I've been thinking about:

- *What was it like for you when you were my age?*
- *What were your struggles, hopes, and dreams? Are you happy or disappointed with the way your life has turned out? What would you do differently?*
- *What helped you find the right track? What were the things that dragged you down?*
- *How did you go about finding out who you are, and what your life is about?*
- *Has anyone else ever felt the same things I'm feeling, or am I just different?*
- *What were, and are, your views about dating and sex? What should I be looking for in a woman? How old were you when you got married? How long did you date? How long were you engaged? How many different girls did you date? How did you know mom was the "right one"? What did your dad tell you about all this?*
- *How did you decide whether to go to college or not? How did you pick your school? Should I go to college? What should I expect if I go off to college? What are the dangers? What are the opportunities? Is it true that universities cause many students to abandon their religious faith? What kinds of things can I do to get good grades and make the most*

of my college experience? What would you suggest? How do I determine what I should major in?

- How do I determine what kinds of careers I might be good at doing?
- How do I learn to keep and balance a checkbook? How do I learn to spend money wisely?
- How did you decide how many children to have? What advice do you have for a son starting a family of his own?
- How did you pick your friends? How can I maintain meaningful friendships, and do I need to?
- What does it mean to be a true Christian? How do you feed your soul? Can I be a Christian and still have fun? What's the big deal about church? Why are there so many hypocrites? Do you believe the Bible is true?
- How should I interpret my emotions and moods?
- What's the best way to organize my life for success? How can I set reasonable expectations?
- What am I to think of all the suffering and evil in the world? How should I handle my own disappointments?
- What are the things that are most important to you—your values, and how did you pick them?
- Have you ever made a written plan for your life? Should I? What would it look like? Is this something you could help me with?

> Has anyone else ever felt the same things I'm feeling, or am I just different?

I was really hoping that you could help me sort this out. Would that be a possibility? Maybe I wouldn't be a very good student and listener, but I think if I had the chance I might surprise you. I admire you a lot, even though I probably don't act like it at times. I love you, Dad, and want to get to know you more—man to man. Would you be open to spending some time with me to figure myself out?

Love,

Michael

Q *Which parts of this letter capture how you feel, and why?*
How do you feel differently, and why?
What's the biggest personal challenge you are
feeling right now?

Three Things All Men Want

After twenty-eight years of helping men think more deeply about Christ and life, I find men basically want three main things:

1. *Something we can give our lives to*—a cause or mission. This is the need to be significant, to make a difference. A man wants his life to count. He wants it to matter that he existed.

2. *Someone to share it with.* This is the need to love and be loved, to be part of a community, to find acceptance, to have healthy relationships. By nature men want a woman to love, protect, and provide for—we want someone to share our lives with.

3. *A "system" ("story" or "worldview") that offers a reasonable explanation for why 1 and 2 are so difficult.* Life is difficult and, for sanity's sake, we each need a plausible explanation of how the bits and pieces of life all fit together.

Manhood, then, is finding something we can give ourselves to, someone to share it with, and a system that explains how to make sense of our lives. In this book we will explore how to satisfy these three God-given desires that men have.

Q *Which of these three desires is most on your mind right now, and why?*

The Need to Be Significant

In the movie *Pearl Harbor*, Colonel Dolittle, a famous pilot, inspires a group of young men to accept a secret mission. They all leap at the opportunity. Only *after* they all sign up does one young pilot say, "We might die for this. We at least want to know what it's for."

> "To be a man is to spend yourself in a worthy cause."

In many ways this scene captures the essence of what it means to be a man. Easily the most distinguishing characteristic of a man is his desire to spend himself in a worthy cause—to make a contribution. And as the movie scene suggests, it is not unlike a man to be so hungry to give his life to a great cause, that he will accept a mission that might cost his life—without even knowing why!

This most distinguishing characteristic of a man is captured by the phrase, "I want to do something with my life." A man's greatest need is his need to be significant—to do something with his life.

A man wants his life to count, to make a difference, to have purpose, to have meaning, to make a contribution, to do something worthwhile. Man is made for a mission, a cause, a task. He wants it to matter that he existed. One of the greatest regrets older men feel is, "My life didn't matter."

When my son left for college I tried to think of a final piece of advice I could give him. I found myself saying, "John, the men I work with often say that when they were young they merely 'played a role' they thought would make other people happy or get them where they wanted to go. Basically, they pretended. Then, when they reached about thirty-five years of age they realized they had not lived an authentic life. I want to encourage you not to settle for anything less than all God wants you to be. Take this time now to discover who you really have been created to be."

If you settle, you will probably wake up one day in your mid-thirties and realize that you got what you wanted, but you sold your soul to get it. Instead of "doing something with your life" for God's glory, you merely got *rich* or *famous* or *comfortable*.

No man wants to fail. No man wakes up in the morning and thinks to himself, *I wonder what I can do today to mess up my life?* But it happens.

A lot of men give the best years of their lives to ideas that never had any chance of helping them become the men God created them to be. Often, it's simply because they did not have someone come alongside and mentor them.

Q *"The distinguishing characteristic of a man is captured by the phrase, 'I want to do something with my life.' A man's greatest need is his need to be significant— to do something with his life." Does this ring true to you or not, and why?*

How badly do you want to be an authentic man and do something with your life?

A Challenge

A man once told me, "Under certain circumstances I would be willing to die for you." Where does that come from? There is a noble impulse to manhood inside each of us.

Besides different anatomy, a man has different instincts than a woman. By nature men are drawn to gather, hunt, explore, adventure, and conquer—we want to give ourselves to a mission. Why do young men dream about becoming explorers, discoverers, adventurers, warriors, and knights? It is because we each have been made to spend ourselves in a worthy cause.

This is a book to help initiate you into manhood. You are being "asked up" into manhood. Because you are becoming a man, you need to know what a man is made to do. Are you ready to accept this challenge?

Q *Are you ready to be "asked up" into manhood?*

PART

2 | DIRECTION

3 | finding a "system" that makes sense of your life

I think I know why I quit high school. My teachers were terrific at explaining their own fields, but nobody pulled all of that diversity into a unified "whole." In short, I didn't have a system (synonyms: story, worldview).

Scholar Neil Postman wrote, "Human beings require stories to give meaning to the facts of their existence. . . . The young need a story [sometimes called a *narrative, meta-narrative,* or *worldview*] to help them sort through the collection of disconnected, fragmented diploma requirements that is called a curriculum." A story provides "a kind of theory about how the world works—and how it needs to work if we are to survive."[1]

All nations that have recorded their histories have used stories. For what? To help them tie the bits and pieces of their lives together. Stories pass the great and noble ideas from generation to generation. Stories help us remember where we're from.

A story is a map that shows you how to walk into the future by checking with reference points from the past. Stories are like a baton that gets passed from my generation to your generation. Stories are a sort of glue that holds civilizations together. They are the ligaments of any "system"

> *Human beings require "stories" to give meaning to the facts of their existence.*

that attempts to explain why finding *something we can give our lives to* and *someone to share it with* are so difficult.

All stories (worldviews, theories, religions, philosophies, systems) try to answer the same questions:

- What does it mean to be a human being? (This is "anthropology"—the study of the origin, nature, and destiny of human beings.)
- Origin: a useless passion evolved from a monkey, or created by God in his image?
- Nature: basically good, or sinful needing salvation?
  - Destiny: rot in the ground, or go into an afterlife?
  - How did we get here?
  - Is there purpose to our existence?
  - What has meaning?
  - What is true?
  - How do we make a contribution?
  - How can we find happiness?
  - What happens when we die?
  - Is there a God?
  - If so, can we know him?

> *Stories are roadmaps to keep you from getting lost. Stories pass great and noble ideas from generation to generation.*

Q *Which of these questions are most on your mind, and why?*

Common Stories

Here are some stories you will see frequently:[2]

The American Dream. This story basically says that if you want something badly enough, *you can do anything if you are willing to pay the price.* This is the rugged individualist, think-positive story.

Technological Paradise. This is the story of *a paradise gained through bigger and better machines* that will ultimately solve the problems humans could not solve.

The Yuppie's Tale. This is the story of my generation. It is the story that *an increasingly greater consumption of goods is beneficial* (consumerism).

Human Progress. The story of the twentieth century—the idea that man is basically good. It is an optimistic story that *the world can be made right if we just try hard enough and work together.*

Science. The story of science rests on the ideas of evolution and chance. To the question, "Where do we come from?" science answers, *"It was an accident."*

> Human Progress is the gospel of "try to be a better person and leave the world a better place."

Postmodernism. We live in what many are calling a "postmodern" world. This story is developing because the "human progress" story did not work out like planned. Many people find our world to be pointless and a place of despair. As one troubled college student told my daughter, "I believe in God, but I think he sucks." Postmodernism questions the possibility of knowing truth (truth is said to be relative), and the significance of human existence. Believers in this story often descend into nihilism, which will be explained further in chapter 4.

Christianity. The Christian story embraces science, technology, progress, prosperity, and optimism. But these are "second things."[3] Christianity is the story of Jesus—his birth, life, work, death, and resurrection. No Jesus, no story. The Christian story promises

1. something you can give your life to
2. someone to share it with
3. a reasonable explanation for why life is so difficult

It is worth noting that Christianity and secular stories (systems) are not trying to solve different problems, but the same problems in different ways.

Here's another way to think about these stories. Most of them are "gospels"—meaning that they offer "good news" about the questions young men ask. They each have prophets, priests, evangelists, and devoted followers.

Q Would you say your peer group is generally pessimistic or optimistic? What stories do the guys in your peer group believe?

Which of these stories is most like the story you have been hearing so far in your life?

Which of these stories do you find most attractive, and why?

Finding a Story That Hangs Together

In some sense all the conflicts and battles of your life are part of your quest to "make sense of your world"—to fit the bits and pieces of your existence into a system, story, or worldview that hangs together.

Why would you challenge authority, question your elders, and resist oversimplified answers like, "Because I said so"? Is it merely because you are a renegade—an unbeliever? No, it is precisely because you are looking for something solid to believe in—something upon which you can build your life—a foundation, a rock, an immovable truth, "a story."

> "Elders, tell us how it all fits together."

Questioning your elders (with respect) is part of the process by which you put your story together. Young men want their elders to not only tell them *what* to do, but *why*, and *how* it fits into the bigger scheme of life.

God made our minds in a way that we want "wholeness." (Psychologists like to call this *gestalt*.) For example, what happens if a friend tells you half of a story about a mutual friend and then decides he shouldn't be telling you? Your mind screams out for what? The rest of the story. Why? Because your mind wants the "whole" story.

We each need a story (system) that is not only true but that makes sense of our lives. The Christian story is so satisfying because it is both true and explains our lives. It hangs together and makes sense of our existence.

Q *Why is it important to find a story that is true? What do we risk if we don't?*

The Christian Man: What's His Story?

Christians have a story—a worldview, a system—that makes sense of life. Christianity promises to give you satisfying answers to the "big questions" about life.

We have a saying in business, "Your system is perfectly designed to produce the result you are getting."[4] If you manufacture cars and every third car that rolls off the assembly line is missing a front right fender, your system is perfectly designed to produce that result. It's the same with our belief systems. They are perfectly designed to produce the results we get, which, of course, is why having the right belief system is so crucial.

In this book I will attempt to show you how Christianity is the story that can best satisfy your desires for meaning, purpose, making a contribution, making a sacrifice for a worthy cause, the happiness we all want, and eternal life (more in chapter 7, "Joining the Revolution").

Are other stories false? No, at least *not completely*. No story would attract any followers unless it at least appeared to explain our lives. The difficulty is that those stories have "enough" truth and make "enough" sense to attract a following, but not enough to fill the hole in your heart. Eventually, they collapse under the weight of a thousand little inconsistencies—often after a man has given that story the best years of his life.

> Unfortunately, this will happen only after you give that story (system) the best years of your life.

Here are some conclusions about other stories compared to the Christian story:

- Most stories *including Christianity* promise salvation and happiness, explain suffering, deal with futility, and attempt to correct the social injustices of the world.
- All stories *except Christianity* and postmodernism do this by trying to re-create or return to "the garden" (utopia).
- All stories *except Christianity* are attempts to save us from "other people's sins." Only Christianity saves us from our "own" sins.
- All stories come to nothing except the Christian story.

The Christian story provides the foundation for human dignity, identity, meaning, purpose, relationships, morality, and a vocation by which a man "does something with his life."

A Challenge

I can't help but wonder if my life would have taken a different course if someone had taken me aside and said . . .

- You need a story to give meaning to the facts of your existence.
- Here are some of the stories that are out there.
- Here's why the Christian story is superior.

Do you know your story? You already have much of it, of course. The challenge of becoming a man includes putting together a story that holds water. Exploring the subjects in this book should be a big help as you organize the bits and pieces of your life to build that story.

Q *Have you ever thought about quitting? If so, why?*

Do you like the idea of building a story or "system," and why or why not?

Do you feel you have a grasp of the Christian story yet? Explain your answer.

> *All stories attempt to save us from other people's sins. Only Christianity saves us from our own sins.*

4 | a man's identity

Recently I spoke to forty young men, ages 14 to 17, in the Orange County, Florida, jail. These boys were major offenders incarcerated for serious crimes: rape, murder, robbery, weapons, and mostly drugs. Ninety percent of them had no father figure. (Ninety-three percent of all people in prison are male, and 85 percent of them have no father figure.)

I was able to keep their attention by telling them about quitting school, and how my brothers have struggled with alcohol, drugs, divorce, and bitterness. Also, I shared the tragic death of my younger brother to a drug and alcohol overdose.

At the beginning of my message I walked around and handed each young man a nametag. Halfway through my talk, I asked each boy to write his name on the tag and stick it to his chest.

Then I went and knelt in front of each boy, one by one, read his nametag, looked him in the eye, and said, "Carlos Rivera (or whatever was on his tag), God knows your name. He loves you very much. He knit you together in your mother's womb. He knows every word you speak before it comes to your tongue. He knows when you sit and when you stand. He knows every-thing you have ever done and will do, and he wants to forgive you. He has good plans for you. If you will reach out for him, he is already reach-ing out for you. You can change your life if you

> 85 percent of these boys have no father figure.

> God loves you
> very much.

want to. God wants to adopt you and be your father. Do you understand this?"

At first I heard a couple of snickers around the room. By the third young man, the snickers gave way to pregnant anticipation. Each time I knelt in front of one of those boys, I could see a thirst in his eyes for encouragement. Each boy looked me directly in the eye as I spoke to him. Like dry sponges, each soaked up what I was telling him about his identity. Every one of them acknowledged that they understood what I was telling them. A few boys didn't put on their nametags. When I came to one of them I quietly said, "Go ahead and put your nametag on, and I'll come back to you." With only enough hesitation to "stay cool," they all did because they all wanted to receive this blessing.

Toward the end I knew that I had missed about three boys. I was pretty sure I knew which ones, but to be absolutely sure I said, "Who have I not spoken to yet?" One young man cried out and pointed to his friend, and said, "You haven't done him yet!" His friend had a sheepish look on his face, but I could tell he really didn't want to miss out.

At the end of my time with them I offered an opportunity for these young men to repent of their sins and put their faith in Jesus Christ. Several did, and several others indicated they already had since coming to jail.

As they were dismissed at the conclusion of my message I said, "I'm a hugger, so if any of you need a hug come up and see me before you leave." Frankly, I'm still not sure why I said that; but the next thing I

> No matter what
> you've done, you
> can be forgiven.

knew, twelve young prisoners had lined up to get a hug. I gave each young man his hug, we exchanged words, and then he went into the hall where guards handcuffed him to another prisoner for the walk back to their cells.

Why did I do this? Sons need the approval of their fathers—sometimes called "the blessing." I'm certainly not qualified to give these boys "the" blessing of a father, but I wanted to give them "a" blessing. I wanted them to know their identity— who they really were created to be. And I wanted them to know Jesus Christ was available to them even though they had done bad things.

> The guards handcuffed the boys to each other for the walk back to their cells.

A lot of our identity comes from our father's blessing. It is his seal of approval. In the Bible, *to bless* means "to endue with power for success, prosperity, fertility, longevity, etc."

In the Old Testament Jacob cheated his older brother, Esau, out of his father's blessing. Their father, Isaac, according to the custom of that time, had to tell Esau that he had already given Esau's blessing to Jacob. The Bible says, "When Esau heard his father's words, he burst out with a loud and bitter cry and said to his father, 'Bless me—me too, my father!'" (Genesis 27:34).

Q *What is a father's blessing, and what does it accomplish? Why do you think receiving a father's blessing is such a big deal?*

Have you received your father's blessing? If that hasn't happened yet or if that's not possible, I would like to give you a blessing.

Read this as though I were God's representative. Receive these words on behalf of God:

"_____ *(write your name here), God knows your name.*

He loves you very much.

He knit you together in your mother's womb.

He knows every word you speak before it comes to your tongue.

He knows when you sit and when you stand. He knows everything you have ever done and will do, and he wants to forgive you.

He has good plans for you.

If you will reach out for him, he is already reaching out for you.

God wants to adopt you and be your True Father. This is your true identity.

You can change your life if you want to.

Do you understand this?"

(Read more about how God made you and knows you in Psalm 139.)

The World on Identity

One hundred years ago at the height of the Scientific and Industrial Revolutions, the world was optimistic that human progress was inevitable—that human ingenuity would solve all the world's problems and eliminate war.

That idea was shattered in the middle years of the twentieth century by two world wars, the genocide of the Jews, the detonation of the atomic bomb, a nuclear arms race, revelations of unspeakable human torture in the labor camps of Russia, and dozens of other atrocities.

After seeing all this, the famous French existential philosopher and atheist Jean Paul Sartre concluded, "Man is an empty bubble with nothing at the center. Man commits himself, draws his portrait, and that's all there is. Life is a useless passion."

The once-optimistic world has become cynical.

A lot of people listened to Sartre (and others like him) because what he said *seemed* to explain what they saw. The world got more pessimistic. But people still wanted to believe in something and have hope, so they tried to "be brave"—meaning they tried to leave the world a better place, even though they stopped thinking they really would.

In recent years the pessimism in some circles has become, if possible, more severe. Many people in our postmodern world think life is such a useless passion that it isn't even worth trying to be brave any longer. They have stopped trying to answer the big questions about life. If the mantra of the modern era was "be brave," the mantra of the postmodern era is "have fun"—meaning they don't care about purpose, the future, success, or doing something with their lives. At best they get by, and often they become a tragic statistic.

A man named Ken Myers made me aware of the following cartoon, which offers an interesting perspective of the modern and postmodern moods:

Modernism   Postmodernism

☹   ☺

Life sucks.   Life sucks.

This is the world's perspective.

How much do you see this postmodern and cynical perspective in your circle of friends?

How much does this perspective resonate with you, and why?

Christianity on Identity

A Japanese teenager who became a Christian said, "A missionary came and told us that we had been created by God. No one had ever told me before that I was created."

Christianity teaches that mankind is the highest expression of God's creativity—that we are creatures created by a great and good Creator. He has made us "like" himself in many ways—in his image or likeness.

King David asked in Psalm 8:3–4:

> When I consider your heavens,
>> the work of your fingers,
> the moon and the stars,
>> which you have set in place,
> *what is man that you are mindful of him,*
>> *the son of man that you care for him?*

He answered the question this way:

> *You made him* a little lower than the heavenly beings
>> and crowned him with glory and honor.
> *You made him* ruler over the works of your hands;
>> you put everything under his feet (Psalm 8:5–6).

God has a "design" or plan for mankind in general, and you in particular. You are special. God loves you very much. You are the full expression of God's creative genius. *God was at his very best when he made you.*

> *"No one had ever told me before that I was created."*

You do not have to "do" anything to be good enough for God to love you, nor can you. God sent Jesus Christ to be "good enough" on your behalf.

The big question about your identity is: Will you see yourself as "a useless passion" or "created in the image of God"?

> *Jesus is good enough.*

Figuring out "who you are" is a lifelong process, but answering this question is the starting point—the first piece of putting together the puzzle.

Your identity, if you are (or become) a Christian man, is based upon who you are *in Christ.* You exist because of and for the glory of Jesus Christ. You will find your identity in a relationship with Jesus Christ. You maintain that relationship through daily renewing yourself in the gospel of Jesus Christ through ongoing repentance and faith.

Q *Have you seen yourself as "a useless passion," "created in the image of God," or something in between? Explain your answer.*
What makes the Christian view of our identity so appealing?

> *"Are you simply trying to say that the best way to find my true identity is to be a Christian? Is that what you're trying to say?"*

A Challenge

We are not finished with the task of identity. For now, though, I would like to ask you to consider some questions:

Q *Are you comfortable with your identity or not, and why?*
Can you write down a sentence that describes "who you are"—a "you" that you like? Write it here if you want:

_____

Where are the "holes" in your identity—the things you have yet to settle?

We will add more pieces to the puzzle as we continue. In the next chapter let's discuss a man's *purpose.*

5 | a man's purpose

Someone has said, "Until you find a cause worth dying for, you will not have a cause worth living for."

A man can't just sit around all day—he would go crazy. He feels compelled to "do something with his life." Women are naturally drawn to relationships and nurturing. Men want a task, a mission, a cause, a purpose. That's a key difference.

When Ernest Shackleton planned his third polar expedition he reportedly ran this ad:

> MEN WANTED for Hazardous Journey. Small wages, bit-
> ter cold, long months of complete darkness, constant dan-
> ger, safe return doubtful. Honour and recognition in case
> of success.

He needed 27 men. five thousand applied. Why? Because men want to do something with their lives that can make a difference.

The Cry of a Man's Heart

Men are created by God to dream dreams. God created us to be hunters, gatherers, adventurers, lovers, and warriors. A man not only wants a hero, he wants to be one. He wants to spend himself in a worthy cause, while soaring.

Deep inside each of us a voice cries out to be heard. I do not want to be taught how to live happily in my cage. I want to soar like an eagle.

I want to run like a tiger. I want to fight like a lion. I want to be free!

What's more, I believe that is my destiny. Every instinct within me screams, "This is why I was made. I was made for a purpose. I was made to soar!"

Are we uneasy because we wonder if this is why we were made? No, we know instinctively that this is why God made us. We are uneasy because we have not yet taken hold of that for which we were created—the reason for our existence.

The story is told about an eagle egg that accidentally ended up in the nest of a prairie chicken. The baby eagle grew up scratching the ground.

One day he looked up and saw a beautiful bird in the sky. He asked his stepmother, "What's that?"

"Oh, that is the majestic eagle, the greatest of all birds."

"I wish I could be like that," he pined.

"Why, you're just a prairie chicken! You will never be like the great eagle. Don't give that another thought!" So he never gave it another thought.

Do you want to be told how to be tame and live in the cage, or do you want God to open the door and set you free?

Kenny said, "I know God loves me. I know that I'm made in his image. But that's kind of static. I need a reason for being here. I need to know why I was born. Why am I here? There must be some purpose to it all."

A life without purpose is like a river without banks. Without riverbanks a river would stop moving forward. It would have no direction. In fact, it would spill out in every direction. In the same way, without a purpose you wouldn't be able to move forward, and you wouldn't have any direction. Knowing the purpose of your life can point you in the right direction and give you some velocity.

> God has a purpose for your life.

If your *identity* is who God created you to "be," then your *purpose* is what God created you to "do."

Look at the verses again from Psalm 8, but this time notice the captions I've inserted:

*Verse 4: What is man that you are mindful of him,
the son of man that you care for him?*

Your Identity: Who God created you to "be"—
*Verse 5: You made him a little lower than the heavenly
beings and crowned him with glory and honor.*

Your Purpose: What God created you to "do"—
*Verse 6: You made him ruler over the works of your hands;
you put everything under his feet.*

Your purpose is *to do something with your life.* It is *the reason you exist.*
It defines your *mission* in life and your *calling.* Your purpose answers life's
larger questions—not "What do I do today?" but . . .

- "Why do I exist?"
- "Why am I here?"
- "What are my functions in life?"
- "What does God want me to do with my life long term?"

In life you will set goals. A purpose is different than a goal. Let's suppose you want to go to college—that's your goal. But why? What is the reason? Your answer is your purpose for wanting to go. For example, it could be as specific as acquiring the skill and training to become an engineer, businessman, or educator. Or, it could be as general as to become equipped for a meaningful career. So a *goal* is something specific you want to accomplish; a *purpose* is *why* you want to accomplish it.

One of the main things you will do over the next few years will be to discover your purpose.

> One of your principal tasks over the next few years will be to discover your life purpose.

How often do you wonder, "Why am I here?"

> *Does your life have riverbanks, and why or why not?*

> *What strikes you most about what is written in Psalm 8?*

37

Four Universal Purposes

There is a sense in which all men are alike, and God gives all men the same universal purposes. The Bible reveals four universal purposes that apply to all men:

1. To love God (The Great Commandment, Matthew 22:37–38)

2. To love others (The New Commandment, Matthew 22:39–40; John 13:34–35)

3. To tend the culture (The Cultural Mandate, Psalm 8:6–8; Genesis 1:28)

This includes our involvement in

- family
- work
- citizenship
- education, arts, law, science, medicine, government, military
- works of justice and mercy

4. To build the kingdom (The Great Commission, Matthew 28:18–20)

This includes our involvement in

- evangelism
- discipleship
- service and missions
- social justice
- meeting the needs of the poor
- a church community

Everything you will ever do in life will fit into one of these four categories.

Your Personal Life Purpose Statement

There is also a sense in which you are unique, and God will give you a personal life purpose. Your personal life purpose is the particular way God intends to weave these four universal purposes together in your life.

What are some examples of personal life purpose statements that men have developed? One man's purpose statement is "To glorify God in all that I do." Another, "To be a man after God's own heart." One man's is, "To be a godly husband, father, churchman, businessman, and citizen." My own written life purpose statement is, "I want to live the rest of my earthly life for the will of God." Notice several things:

> *Your purpose gives you a reason to get out of bed in the morning!*

- They are significant.
- They are long term.
- They are more about the theory of why we exist than specific tasks or short-term roles that may change.
- They are God-centered.
- They are not "what" we do, but "why" we do.
- They are not a "goal," but more like a "guiding star."

Knowing the purpose God has for your life gives you a reason to get out of bed in the morning. It's motivational. It gives you a reason for living. It gives you direction.

Questions you may have:

What time period should my life purpose cover? There are no set rules, but generally think of a life purpose statement as a long-term idea (five years or more for a high school student, ten years or more once you're on your own).

How long will it take to find my personal life purpose, and when will I know I've found it? There is no set schedule. You may already know, but probably not. You may see it, but like a shadowy figure at dawn. It may become more clear by the end of this book, maybe not. You will most likely experience a growing sense of certainty about God's direction for your life, and then, one day, you'll be sure.

> *I'm pretty sure that I would not have quit high school if I had thought my life had a purpose—even if I had not yet discovered what it was.*

A Challenge

You may be surprised to learn that only a few men ever take time to write down a life purpose statement. That doesn't mean men don't act with purpose. It does mean they lack a carefully worded statement to act as sort of a "guiding star" to lead their choices.

Let me ask you to take a few moments right now and reflect on these questions and suggestions:

- "Lord, why do I exist?"
- Think about the four universal purposes God has for all men.
- "What is my personal life purpose right now as a student?"
- Consider noting Bible verses that really speak to you.
- Pray and ask God for wisdom.
- Journal or write down thoughts. A pencil will sharpen your focus.
- If you can, write down a "first draft" sentence that you believe captures the essence of why you exist:

_____

_____

One reason so many men don't "do something with their lives" is that they never really pin down who they are and why they exist. I know it sounds hard to believe, but many men go through life in a fog. They just go through the motions and then, one day, they die. I don't want you to miss all that God has in store for you. Make the effort to think through God's purpose for your life. It can be a defining moment for your life.

> A happy man is a man who knows his purpose.

Q God has a purpose for your life. It is the reason you exist and "do something" with your life. Do you find this exciting, and why or why not?

6 | the story of Jesus

The Christian story is the story of Jesus. Jesus did not come to call men to be *better*. He came to call men to *new life,* a whole new way of thinking. He did not come to start a boy's club—he came to be the founder of a revolution, to take back territory from the enemy, to rescue men's souls from hell. He was a reformer, a radical, a liberator, a Braveheart. Jesus Christ came to start the Revolution.

> *Christianity is the story of Jesus. Jesus is Christianity. He is the whole story.*

Who Is This Man?

In the Bible's Gospels of Matthew, Mark, Luke, and John, we learn "the story" of Jesus.

He was born in poverty. He earned no degrees. He never owned property. He never held public office. He did not command an army. He never traveled more than one hundred miles from his hometown. He never wrote a book. His only possession was the clothing he wore.

He was tempted just like us but never sinned. He said, "Deny yourself, take up your cross,

> *Poor, no formal education, no property or possessions, no office, no army, no book, no television program.*

Jesus knew who
he was and why
he existed.

follow me." He said that nothing is impossible if you have faith (see Matthew 17:20).

A woman ill for many years was healed by merely touching the hem of his robe. He made blind people see. He raised Lazarus from the dead. He walked on water. He multiplied small amounts of fish and bread to feed five thousand.

Jesus understood his *identity*—who he was. He said, "If you have seen me you have seen the Father. The Father and I are one" (John 10:30).

Jesus understood his *purpose*—why he existed. He said, "I came to seek and to save the lost and give my life as a ransom for many" (Luke 19:10).

Jesus sacrificed worldly pleasures for his mission. He was obedient to his Father's will. He did not come to call people who were convinced they were already good. He came to call sinners to repent. He came to give life and give it abundantly to all who will receive him.

Healings, raised
dead, miracles,
obedient,
authority, prayer,
sinless, betrayed,
deserted.

Jesus spoke with authority. He spoke in parables about the kingdom of God. He taught ethics in the Sermon on the Mount. He taught people to love those not naturally their friends—even enemies (which seems hard when they are terrorizing your country). He said, "Unless you change and become like a little child you will not enter the kingdom" (Matthew 18:3). He said, "You must forgive others." He said, "Do not divorce." He said, "It is hard for a rich man to enter the kingdom of heaven."

He often went to quiet places to pray. He taught his disciples how to pray the Lord's Prayer. He wept. He became extremely angry with religious hypocrites. He was extremely patient with his disciples.

The most important religious leaders of the day plotted against him. He was betrayed by one of his closest associates. He was arrested without cause. He was deserted. He was put on trial. Soldiers mocked him and beat him senseless. People spit on him. He was crucified until he was dead. He was buried in a borrowed tomb.

Three days later the stone rolled away. Jesus was resurrected from the dead. He appeared to his disciples and five hundred other witnesses. He told his disciples to tell others of his resurrection. He told his disciples to make other disciples and to teach them to obey his teachings. He ascended into heaven. He will come again.

> *Crucified, dead, buried, resurrected, 40 days, 500 witnesses, ascended, coming again.*

The most successful man who ever lived is Jesus. At his ascension his followers numbered 120 men, yet today over one billion people call him Lord and God.

Of Jesus, Napoleon said, "I die before my time and my body shall be returned to the earth and devoured by worms. I marvel that whereas the ambitious plans of myself and of Caesar and of Alexander should have vanished into thin air, that a Judean peasant, Jesus, should be able to stretch his hands across the ages and control the destinies of men and nations."

Q *Who did Jesus understand himself to be?*
Explain in your own words who Jesus is and why he came.

The Problem Jesus Solves

What is the problem that Jesus solves?

Jewel sings, "We've been given to a God to put our faith therein, but to be forgiven we must first believe in sin."

> *The 9/11 terrorist attacks represent only a small fraction of the evil done each year. For example, over 150,000 Christians are martyred for their faith every year around the world according to the* **World Christian Encyclopedia.**

> You must first
> believe in your
> own sin.

An investigation of the human condition doesn't yield a solution but a problem. Sin. We are caged in a world stricken with sin. We have free will, but we have used it sinfully.

On closer examination we see that the world is stricken not merely by sin but by *our* sin. It is *our* cruelty, *our* selfishness, *our* pride, and *our* mean-spiritedness that is making the world so unbearable.

The first step to getting free from your cage is to understand why you are in there in the first place. You must first believe you are a sinner.

There is a lot of talk these days that what happens to us is not our fault. It's made to sound like we are victims. But what makes a victim a victim is that he had no choice in the matter. Most of the time we do have a choice. What makes a sinner a sinner is choice—a bad choice.

What is the problem Jesus solves?

The Gospel of Jesus

Here are some startling conclusions from Scripture:

- Jesus Christ is the only man who ever lived a righteous life.
- Jesus Christ is the only man who has ever been acceptable to God.
- Nothing we can ever do will make us acceptable to God.
- We are sinners.
- Jesus died for sinners.
- We should stop trying to be good enough for God to love and accept us.
- God loves Jesus and accepts him.
- When through repentance we "graft" ourselves into Christ by faith and abide in him (like branches to a vine), we become acceptable to God.

- The righteousness of Jesus is given to us, and we are saved by faith.
- It is never our righteousness, but the righteousness of Jesus.

God loves you very much. He has not left us alone, but sent his son Jesus Christ into the world to save sinners like us. Jesus lived a holy, blameless, righteous life. Jesus never sinned but willingly died as a substitute for anyone who will trust him.

The Bible puts it this way: "But now a righteousness from God, apart from law, has been made known, to which the Law and the Prophets testify. This righteousness from God comes through faith in Jesus Christ to all who believe. There is no difference, for all have sinned and fall short of the glory of God, and are justified freely by his grace through the redemption that came by Christ Jesus. God presented him as a sacrifice of atonement, through faith in his blood" (Romans 3:21–25).

Here is an amazing thing: Jesus did not come to look for good people that he could save because they were good. Jesus came to seek out bad people and save them in spite of their sinfulness.

The gospel is the good news (story) that God has entered history in the person of Jesus to renew the whole world and set men free who have been caged by sin. When we believe and rely on the work and record of Jesus rather than our own record, we enter into a personal relationship with God, *the Revolution takes place,* and we become a "new creation" (2 Corinthians 5:17)— prepared to do something with our lives that will matter.

Write here why Jesus came:

_____
_____
_____
_____
_____
_____
_____
_____

What kind of people did he come for?

_____

A Strange Thing

The strange thing about Christianity is that it transforms the lives of men *not by appealing to our human will* but by telling a story; *not by exhortation* but by the narration of an event.

Sure, such a method seems strange. What could be more impractical than trying to talk you into joining the Revolution by rehearsing the events surrounding the death of a religious teacher? But the strange thing is that it works. The effects of it appear all over the world. Where the most eloquent exhortation fails, the simple story of an event succeeds. The lives of men are transformed by a piece of news.[5]

What is it about the story of Jesus that you find intriguing?

A Challenge

All stories are written to men trapped in cages of futility and sin. All stories tell men how they can be free. Yet all stories except the Christian story merely move a man from a cage of one sort to a cage of a different sort. But the soul remains caged—in *bondage*.

Only the Christian story frees the soul from its bondage. *In Christianity, "the person" matters.* Man is important to God. Christian writer G. K. Chesterton pointed out that our "personality" is the purpose of God, the whole point of his cosmic idea! All the philosophies of the world are chains that keep the cages locked. But Christianity is "a sword that smashes the chains and sets us free."[6]

> Your purpose gives you a reason to get out of bed in the morning!

As Jesus himself said, "So if the Son sets you free, you will be free indeed" (John 8:36).

Q To what degree do you feel trapped by a sense of futility and sin?

Do you believe that Jesus can set your free? Explain your answer.

7 | joining the revolution

In the last chapter, I explained what all the fuss is about Jesus. In this chapter I want to invite you to join the Revolution.

Revolution, rebellion, and reform are ideas that appeal to Bravehearts.

The problem is not that young men rebel against the bankrupt values of their parents' generation. The problem is that they have not rebelled far enough.

Writer Mardi Keyes notes that when a young man says "a pox on the adult world and its stupid values," it is a superficial rebellion. Why? Because often young men merely exchange one set of idols for another. What's needed is a much deeper rebellion—one that can only come by allegiance to a truly alternative "counter culture."[7]

A lot of young men have the mistaken idea that Christianity is merely about "behavior modification." They hear, "Change your behavior, be a good boy, do better next time, and you will be saved."

That is not the gospel of Jesus Christ. That is not the Christian story. That is a performance-based Christianity that is not Christianity at all. We do not get out of the cage by changing our behavior. We get out of the cage by joining the Revolution.

> *What's needed is a rebellion of a deeper sort—a complete change of allegiance.*

> We are not set free by changing our behavior. We are set free when we join the Revolution that Jesus founded.

Our youth pastor's theme is, "We want to teach our youth that Christianity is not about being *better*—it's about being *different*." That's it! That's the Revolution, and it is a rebellion of a much deeper kind.

How to Join the Revolution

Many men—young and old, churched and unchurched—have not properly understood what we've discussed about Christianity, Jesus, and the Revolution he began.

It isn't so much that they have rejected the Christian story. Rather, they have never properly understood it. Once understood, however, many men would eagerly embrace Christianity.

Where do you stand with Jesus Christ? Have you properly understood what Christianity is all about? If you have not joined the Revolution, or if you have stumbled and need restoration, this chapter explains how you can embrace Jesus Christ.

There are three questions you must answer to join Jesus' Revolution:

1. "Is it true?"
2. "Do I believe it?"
3. "Will I let it change my life?"

"Is it true?"

Is it true that God loves you, that Jesus is God's son, that God sent Jesus to die for your sins, that he justifies (saves) you from your sins when you have faith in his death and resurrection on your behalf?

> The Christian story is not about being better. It is about being different.

Every man wants to do something with his life. A lot of men, though, give up that dream when the sin of the world starts to eat away at their souls. Other stories promise to remove the sting of the world and the prick of its thorns. Christianity makes no such claim. In fact, Christianity claims that we will see exactly what we see—a fallen world full of death and decay.

No doubt that's why Jesus says, "In this world you will have trouble. But take heart! I have overcome the world" (John 16:33).

Jesus also said, "Come to me, all you who are weary and burdened, and I will give you rest. Take my yoke upon you and learn from me, for I am gentle and humble in heart, and you will find rest for your souls" (Matthew 11:28–29).

God offers eternal life through Jesus: "For God so loved the world that he gave his only Son, so that everyone who believes in him will not perish but have eternal life" (John 3:16).

> Christians are not surprised by evil. Christianity claims we will see exactly what we see.

Jesus promised that "in him" you would be able to do something with your life that counts: "If a man remains in me and I in him, he will bear much fruit; apart from me you can do nothing. . . . This is to my Father's glory, that you bear much fruit, showing yourselves to be my disciples" (John 15:5, 8).

You must decide if you think what Jesus said, did, and promised is true. You have the power of making that choice.

Q Do you think the Christian story is true? Explain your answer.

"Do I believe it?"

The story of Jesus is the story of God reducing himself to flesh so that we might comprehend him. It is either true or it isn't, and we either believe it or we don't. To "believe" means to "put your trust in" Jesus.

Becoming a Christian is starting a personal relationship with Jesus by doing two things—repenting and believing. It is not merely believing that you are a sinner—it is genuine sorrow over it, which is repentance.

THE YOUNG MAN IN THE MIRROR

It is not merely believing that Jesus is Savior and Lord but faith that you want Jesus to save you, lord over you, and be your King. Jesus did not come merely to be an *example* for our faith; he is the *object* of our faith.[8]

Q Do you believe in it? Explain your answer.

"Will I let it change my life?"

How can the gospel story of Jesus change your life? When you repent and put faith in Jesus, he reaches down and unfastens the latch to the cage. He breathes on you, and you are changed. The prairie chicken suddenly realizes that he is an eagle. But there is work to do—you need a change of heart. You have been in the habit of scratching around, and now Jesus will teach you to soar.

Christianity is not "behavior modification"—a change of behavior that leads to a change of heart. Christianity is a change of heart that leads to a change of behavior.

Q Are you willing to let Christ change your life, and why or why not?

A Challenge

If you have not joined the Revolution and are ready to let Jesus change your life, you can embrace him right now through prayer. You can pray in your own words, or you can pray the following prayer. You can pray silently or out loud. Those things don't matter. What matters is the sincerity of your heart.

Apart from Jesus no man will ever be able to do anything of lasting significance with his life.

Lord Jesus, I want to soar. I want to do something with my life. I want to know the reason for which you created me. Yet I know that I am a sinner, and that my sins have

54

caused you sorrow. I'm sorry. Please forgive me and come into
my life by faith. I thank you for forgiving my sins by dying on
the cross for me. I invite you to breathe on me and change me.
Let me become a man of God—a true Christian. Amen.

If you have prayed this prayer for the first time, welcome to the Revolution and the family of God. If perhaps you prayed as a way of rededicating your life to Jesus, then allow Jesus to be your Lord and change your heart.

Have you joined the Revolution? Have you through repentance and faith invited Jesus to be your Savior, Lord, and King?

> *Christianity is the story of Jesus reducing himself to human flesh so that we might comprehend him.*

HEALTHY RELATIONSHIPS

8 | dating

"I love you," said Michael as he stroked Sara's hair. "You make me feel like nobody else ever has." Sara was glad they had each other.

Michael really did care for Sara, but in his heart he knew he was using her. Sara had given him her heart, but he didn't love her the way he made it sound. He couldn't understand why he kept telling her lies, except that he liked getting physical with Sara.

Michael's dad routinely broke his promises to the family. He couldn't remember the last time his dad had initiated a family conversation or activity. As far as Michael was concerned, that was normal. It was the only example he had ever seen.

For her part, Sara really responded to Michael's words of affection. Sara did not get much attention at home. Her mom was always busy with a project, and her dad was rarely around. His job took him out of town several nights each week. When he was at home, he was glued to ESPN.

One weekend Sara tried to strike up a conversation with her dad. She said, "You know, Dad, I was thinking. Maybe you and I could go to a movie together tonight."

"I'm sorry, Sara," her dad said. "I've got some guys coming over to play cards tonight. Maybe another time."

> *"I'm sorry, Sara," her dad said. "Maybe another time." "Sure, Dad, maybe another time."*

"Sure, Dad, maybe another time."

That night after a movie Sara and Michael drove to a park where a lot of the kids from their school hung out. Michael really didn't know what normal behavior toward a woman looked like. Like his dad, he just survived on instinct and wits.

Since he really wanted to have sex with Sara he told her, "I love you so much. I always want us to be together." He was the only man who had shown her any love and affection in a long time. At that moment, Sara made her choice. She would give her love to Michael in whatever way he wanted.

Two and a half months later a trembling Sara met Michael in the parking lot before school and said three words he never dreamed he would hear, "Michael, I'm pregnant."

"What!? Are you sure? I mean, couldn't there be some mistake?"

"It's no mistake, Michael. I'm sure."

They both sat down on a bench and sat for several minutes in stunned silence. Finally Michael said, "Sara, my dad is going to kill me. Do your parents know yet?"

"No, but they're going to kill me too. Michael, you're the only person in my life that I can really count on. What are we going to do?"

Michael thought to himself, *What are we going to do? Good question. I have no idea what we are going to do. I can't believe this is happening. I mean, this wasn't in the plan.*

Q *How close does this story come to describing what you see going on?*

Why Dating Is Such a Big Deal

One of the biggest dating issues in recent years has been whether to "kiss dating goodbye" or "give dating a chance." The issue hasn't been *how* to date, but *whether* to date at all.

The debate was spawned by the book *I Kissed Dating Goodbye* by Joshua Harris. Others responded with counterpoints, notably Jeremy Clark in *I Gave Dating a Chance*.

> *Giving your heart to a young woman creates one set of problems if you stay together, and another set of problems if you break up.*

What's the issue these books are addressing? The issue is "giving your heart" to another person. Whether or not to date is such a big issue because the stakes of giving your heart away are so high, as illustrated in the story above. It is true that all sin can be forgiven. But the consequences of some sins just go on and on and on.

Why is giving your heart to someone such a big issue? Basically, "giving your heart" to a woman is what happens when you meet the woman you want to marry. It is the same thing as falling in love. Once you give your heart to a woman, you have "married" her *emotionally*.

Suppose you are dating and give a young woman your heart. This creates one set of problems if you stay together, and another set of problems if you break up.

If you stay together you have done everything a married couple would do except consummate the marriage *physically*. Once you give your heart to a woman emotionally, the body wants to follow. The desire and the pressure to have sex will be overwhelming. And even if you believe intercourse before marriage is wrong, you will still be under tremendous pressure to do everything else from sexual touching of private parts to oral sex. One small problem. You are not married. It's hard enough for an engaged couple to wait—and they have a wedding date they can look forward to.

> *Once you give your heart to a woman emotionally, the body wants to follow.*

On the other hand, if you break up, the heart goes through the same pain as a married couple getting a divorce.

So it's frustration or failure if you stay together, and a broken heart if you don't.

So why have youth workers made such a big issue about whether or not to date? Both sides have the same goal in mind: to spare you and her many sorrows.

Perhaps that's why it says three times in the Song of Solomon, "I want you to promise me, O women of Jerusalem, not to awaken love until the time is right" (Song of Solomon 2:7, 3:5, 8:4 NLT).

Your parents or her parents—maybe both—have probably invested a lot of love, instruction, and prayer into your lives. So, whether you decide to date or not, guard your heart until you meet the woman you want to marry.

Q *What does it mean to "give your heart" to a woman?*

Is Dating Right for You?

One young man asked, "Should I date? Is it really that important?" There is no one right answer to the dating question, biblically speaking.

A woman is a glorious creature to behold. God did good when he made women. It seems natural that a young man would want to spend some time with one of them.

> *It's frustration or failure if you stay together, and a broken heart if you don't.*

Personally, I think dating is fine. I don't think it makes any difference whether or not you date. The issue is to guard your heart, and I think you can do that either way. Is there risk? Sure. Is dating worth the risk? Sure.

Q *How do you feel about dating? How do your parents feel? Are you on the same page?*

Answering Your Questions

- *Should Christians date non-Christians?* Usually not, and definitely not if your hope is that by dating you they will become Christians (sometimes called "missionary" dating).

- *When is it right to start dating?* Probably not before you are least fifteen, although you may be mature enough to hang out at the mall and go to movies in groups if you're under fifteen. You need to submit to your parents' discretion on this.

- *Isn't dating pointless unless I am ready to get married?* Dating can be an excellent way to learn about the differences between men and women, as well as different personalities and temperaments. Often you will learn what you want in a future mate by learning what you don't want.

> *Personally, I think dating is fine. The issue is to guard your heart.*

- *Do you think people should be in serious dating relationships in high school?* A few couples who start dating in high school end up getting married later (my son, for one). It is not the norm, and most professionals generally recommend against it. If you decide to date one girl exclusively, however, definitely don't give each other your hearts.

- *What should I look for in a date?* Look for someone who loves Christ, has a good family, and one you find yourself drawn toward.

- *How do I find the right girl for me?* That's the fun part of dating. Once you start dating, go out with lots of different types of girls. If you are like one of your parents, think about his or her partner. Would someone with that temperament be a good fit for you? If your parents get along, probably.

- *When is it right to get physically involved (not sex, but stuff like kissing and things)?* A kiss is a special sensation. There is no one right answer, but I would suggest you wait until you have been out several times, then give her a goodnight kiss at her doorstep when you take her home.

- *How far is too far?* Touching breasts or feeling below the waist is too far. A lazy review of the Bible can yield a long list of dos and don'ts. But you already basically know those things. I'll say more on this in the next chapter.

- *How do I keep the relationship from becoming too physical?* Don't be places where getting too physical is possible. If you do go out alone with a girl, decide in advance what your boundaries are for touching, kissing, holding hands, and being alone in any place where sexual activity of any kind could happen.

- *How do I treat a girl with respect?* The main thing in dating is integrity. A former United States senator said, "If you have integrity, nothing else matters. If you don't have integrity, nothing else matters."

The parents of any girl you date have either made a huge investment in that heart, or they have misjudged its value to God and have not. If they have invested in her heart, they have the same hopes that you will one day have for your own children. They love her, hope for her best, and have poured their lives into preparing her for a good life. Would you ruin all that? If they have not invested in her heart, it will be an especially hungry heart, and therefore vulnerable.

> *Often you will learn what you want in a future mate by learning what you don't want.*

- *Who can keep me accountable in a dating relationship, other than my girlfriend?* Good question. Find a like-minded friend and hold each other accountable. Ask each other, "Are you treating _____ with complete integrity? Have you done anything you wouldn't want someone to do to your sister?" That will cover it.

> *Have you done anything you wouldn't want someone to do to your sister?*

- *What can I do to create a good dating relationship?* Be kind, listen, and be a gentleman. Girls are more interested in good qualities than good looks. The secret of successful dating is to not give your heart away, treat your date the way you would want your sister treated, and to be a man of integrity.

- *How do I handle a bad dating relationship?* It depends upon what you mean by bad. But if you are quarreling a lot, you should probably stop the relationship.

- *Should I be old-fashioned (always pay, drive, open door, get chair, give jacket, etc.)?* Eventually you will want a wife and she will want to be married to a gentleman, so go ahead and practice now. About who pays, there is no one right answer. Dutch is fine but, personally, I would pay (then everyone knows that it really is a date).

- *How do I choose between two girls if I like both of them?* You don't have to choose. Go out with both of them, but don't give either your heart.

- *What should I do if her parents don't let her date?* I know this feels like a cookie in a jar you are not supposed to touch. But you have a duty to honor her parents' wishes.

- *Is dating acceptable in the eyes of God if the girl I'm interested in is currently with someone else?* Not if the guy she's dating is unaware.

Again, integrity is everything. By the way, is the kind of girl who would go out behind her boyfriend's back the kind of girl you want?

- *How can I not let dating control my relationships with my friends?* Establish amounts of time you will date, then stick to it.
- *How do I honor my sisters in Christ by "guarding" both of our hearts?* Talking it over is a good place to start, but don't worry about it until you have gone out more than once or twice.
- *When a girl starts out as my best friend but the relationship goes further, how do I work with that?* If a friendship starts to turn into a romance, talk over the idea of not giving your hearts to each other.
- *Where do I draw the line with girl relationships, and how do I control my emotions?* If you don't want to get more involved with a girl, be sure to let your intentions be known early on. As far as controlling your emotions, we'll talk about that in the next chapter.

Q *Is there anything in the Bible that prohibits dating? What cautions would the Bible have (for example, see Ephesians 5:3 and 1 Corinthians 6:18)? Why do you think adults are so concerned about dating?*

> *Eventually you will want a wife, and she will want to be married to a gentleman, so go ahead and practice now.*

A Challenge

Make a commitment as a man of integrity, whether you date or not, to treat all women with the respect you would want for your own sister. Pledge to yourself that you will not give your heart to a woman until you are ready to pursue marriage.

CHAPTER

9 | sex

When James was twelve he was helping his mom clean the closets. He stumbled onto a stack of *Playboy* magazines that his seventeen-year-old brother had squirreled away behind a pile of old clothes.

At first he was shocked that his older brother would be looking at pictures of naked women. Then he got angry. He thought, *I can't believe he would do this! I mean, he's an officer in the youth group at church.*

Next came disgust and a feeling of self-righteousness that he would never stoop to collecting *Playboy* magazines. Next came curiosity—he had never really seen a picture of a naked woman. He opened one of the magazines to the centerfold and felt dizzy. He felt alarms and bells going off inside his head. His chest started heaving up and down as he gasped for breath. As his religious training worked on his conscience, he felt nauseated.

James quietly put the magazines back behind the old clothes and didn't mention a word about them.

For the rest of the week he couldn't stop thinking about the way those pictures made him feel. On one hand, he knew it was wrong and it made him feel dirty. On the other hand, he had never felt such strong feelings.

A week later, when the rest of the family was not home, James snuck back into his brother's

> *He opened one of the magazines to the centerfold and felt dizzy.*

closet to look at more pictures. Over the next couple of months James got hooked. He started masturbating as he looked at the naked women. When he was done he felt guilty. He knew he was doing something he shouldn't do, but he was way too embarrassed to be able to talk to anyone about it. So he found himself in a constant tug of war between knowing what he shouldn't be doing and doing it anyway.

Over the next year James figured out that his brother was into all kinds of pornography and more. He found his brother's tracks on the Internet history pages of the home computer they shared. He found a slip of paper from a clinic that showed his brother had been tested for STDs (sexually transmitted diseases).

James knew that several of the new "friends" his brother had collected were drinking and doing drugs. Also, he saw his once outgoing brother slowly become sullen and withdraw into himself. He was grumpy with the family, and never around much. Things finally came to a head, though, when his brother was accused of trying to use a date rape drug on a girl from school. James was wise enough to see where following in his brother's footsteps would lead. He realized that he could easily be next.

James knew he had a decision to make. Would he lead a secret life of sexual lust, fantasy, and sexual immorality like his brother? Or would he learn God's plan for his sexuality and let God help him control his sexual drive?

Q How close to home does this story hit?
How is sex corrupted in our culture?

Why Wait?

One young man asked, "What things should someone my age know about sex?" Another wanted to know, "If sex is so good, why should we have to wait?" Good questions.

The Bible teaches that sex is an altogether good thing. Sex is one of God's greatest gifts to the human race when it is used according to his plan.

God created sex for two purposes: to make babies and for a married couple to enjoy physical intimacy with each other.

St. Augustine wrote that everything bad is a corruption of something that was originally meant to be good. When sex is used outside of God's plan, a lot of things can and do go wrong.

Sex is a "good." When this good is corrupted, bad things can happen including sexually transmitted diseases (some of which are incurable—approximately 1 of every 3 adults has an incurable STD), infertility, cervical cancer, AIDS, loss of reputation, depression, discipline from God, and pregnancy out of marriage.

Actually, God does not put limits on sex. He puts limits on sexual immorality.

Actually, God does not put limits on sex. He puts limits on sexual immorality.

Since sex is for propagating the human race, women get pregnant—and they don't have to be married or over twenty-one. Many families know the pain caused by teen pregnancy. God can redeem it, but I'm old enough to have seen it create a lot of sadness. Often, an unplanned pregnancy defines who people become—even in my own extended family.

The decisions raised by an unexpected teen pregnancy are overwhelming:

- Does the girl drop out of school?
- Does the girl go away for a while until she has the baby?

- Do you abort? (Christians believe this is murder.)
- Do you put the baby up for adoption?
- If the child is kept, who will be the primary caregivers?
- Will the grandparents alter their lifestyle to help?
- Where will the money come from?
- Will the father be involved, or does he disappear?
- If the father is willing to be involved in parenting, is the mother willing to let him?

> *The number one reason God has guidelines for human sexuality is that sex works very well for its principal purpose—making babies.*

Unfortunately, these potential consequences never occur to many young people until they have to make real decisions about real pregnancy. The number one reason God has guidelines for human sexuality is that sex works very well for its principal purpose—making babies.

Q Why is sexual sin so serious, both spiritually and practically speaking?

How would you handle it if you got a girl pregnant?

What would you do if you got an STD?

Questions about Sex

- *Is it wrong to have premarital sex if I really love the person?* Yes. Sex is intended by God to be between one man and one woman within marriage.
- *Is it wrong to have oral sex before marriage?* Yes. The Bible teaches that our entire bodies and the bodies of young women are temples of God's Holy Spirit. First Corinthians 6:13, 18–20 says, "The body is not meant for sexual immorality, but for the Lord, and the Lord for the body. . . . Flee from sexual immorality. All other sins a man commits are outside his body, but he who sins

sexually sins against his own body. Do you not know that your body is a temple of the Holy Spirit, who is in you, whom you have received from God? You are not your own; you were bought at a price. Therefore honor God with your body."

- *How far is too far?* Touching her breasts or feeling below her waist is too far. Having her touch you below the waist is too far. Rubbing your bodies together, even if clothed (humping, dry sex), is too far. Talking in a way intended to arouse sexual desire in a woman or anything a woman does to intentionally arouse sexual desire in you is too far.

> *How far is too far?*

- *If I have already gone too far, what can I do to correct it?* If you have given your heart to a young woman and you have had intercourse, you will find it difficult to stop. The best thing to do would be to stop the relationship, repent, and submit to a confidential restoration process with a spiritual mentor like your youth pastor. Next best is to agree together that you want to honor God by abstaining, confess and repent together, then do not allow yourselves to ever be in a place private enough that you could fall again. You should tell someone and ask them to hold you accountable. God forgives, but he also expects us to change by relying upon common sense and the power of his Holy Spirit within us.

- *Is it a sin to masturbate? Is masturbation wrong if I feel it can give me more strength when I go out with my girlfriend (strength to not sin with her)?* The Bible does not specifically address masturbation, which is interesting because it easily could have. The Bible does say to avoid sexual immorality or impurity. When puberty begins, at age thirteen or so, your body begins to produce testosterone, the male hormone that makes men aggressive.

Testosterone produces a sexual drive in a man. Testosterone makes men horny. It is normal to want to masturbate. I wouldn't worry too much about it with this caution: Try not to fantasize about women and intercourse. Do not look at pictures of women or stimulate yourself. Second, don't allow yourself to compulsively masturbate. Certainly masturbating several times a week would be considered compulsive.

- *Are the swimsuit edition magazines and Victoria's Secret catalogs pornographic? Should I be looking at them?* They are not pornographic for the girls who look at them, but they are for the boys because the only reason a boy would look at those pictures is for sexual stimulation.

- *How do I defeat lust? How do I control my sex thoughts and actions? How can I keep from getting in sexually tempting situations?* Lust is sexual desire out of control. That desire is aroused in men mostly by sight. The best way to control yourself is to decide in advance what kind of a man you want to be. Then, don't put yourself in situations that you find tempting. For example, ask your mother to screen your mail for sexually explicit materials—like the *Sports Illustrated* swimsuit edition. Don't sit on the beach and stare at girls.

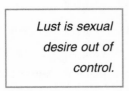

Lust is sexual desire out of control.

- *Is there something wrong with me if I have an erection several times a day?* (No one asked this question in my research, but I know it's on your mind.) It is normal to have an erection (hard penis) as many as several times a day. Erections can result from seeing a girl you find attractive, smelling perfume, a girl touching your arm, a girl's hair brushing against you, or even reading these words. This is normal, not lust. There is nothing wrong with you. On the other hand, having an erection because you are seeking sexual stimulation is lust. For example, seeking out pornography is lust (sexual desire out of control), whether it's underwear ads in the newspaper or an Internet site.

- *Why is it wrong to look at pornography?* Because it arouses sexual desire based upon sexual fantasy. According to the Center for Decency nearly a third (31 percent) of kids ages 10–17 from households with computers (24 percent of all kids 10–17) say they have seen a pornographic Web site.

- *Is homosexuality a sin?* Whether a man has a predisposition to homosexuality or not, homosexual activity is sin. Another man may have a predisposition to theft or alcoholism, but we wouldn't tell him those are not sins.

- *How should I treat women if I don't have a male figure to show me?* Treat them like your own sister. Watch how other men whom you respect treat women.

Q *How far is too far?*

A Challenge

One day you will probably marry. Marriage is the most wonderful relationship in God's order of things. Christian writer G. K. Chesterton put it this way: "Keeping to one woman is a small price for so much as seeing one woman." Until you are ready for marriage, do not ask for, and do not accept, someone's heart. It is too great a responsibility.

> Marriage is the most wonderful relationship in God's order of things.

As a man you have the main responsibility to be a leader in your relationships with women. Women are more vulnerable in matters of the heart than men for two reasons. First, while a man's greatest need is to do something significant with his life, a woman's greatest need is for intimacy. Intimacy is that state when a couple can say to each other, "I know who you are at the very deepest level, and I accept you as you are." Second, if a young woman is not receiving affection at home she is even more vulnerable.

Q *What is the challenge for dating and sex, and will you accept it?*

10 | family relationships

When Spencer asked his mother if he could go with his friends to a music concert in a city two hours down the interstate, she flatly said, "No, Spencer, you can't go."

He said, "But Mom, all my friends are going. Come on, Mom—why won't you let me go? You keep trying to hold me back like I was still in middle school. Can't you see that I'm growing up?

> "You don't trust me."

You don't trust me. It's just not fair. Dad would let me go if he were here."

"Well, your dad isn't here, and I'm trying to do the best I can. Spencer, I do trust you, but I just don't think you're ready yet."

When Spencer thought about going to the concert and staying out late he pictured adventure, excitement, friends, and fun. When his mom thought about it she pictured bad people, drugs, drunk drivers, accidents, and ambulances.

Q *Is this realistic? Would this happen in your family? How would you handle the situation?*

The Brother

"You stupid little worm," said Cameron. "How many times have I told you to stay out of my CDs?"

> Worm.
> Jerk.
> Creep.

"I didn't do anything, you jerk," his younger brother responded.

Cameron was ready. "You see that matchstick on the floor? I had that stuck in the lid to my CD holder. It's on the floor because you've been in my CDs again. I find you guilty as charged."

And then he slugged his brother on the arm, which gave him a sense of justice and his brother a bruise—though his brother refused to cry.

Then Cameron said, "You have the right to remain stupid. Anything you say can and will not be remembered. If you tell Dad I hit you I'm going to flush your goldfish down the toilet. Do you understand?"

"Yeah, yeah . . . you creep."

How often does this happen in your family? Do these conflicts get resolved or swept under the rug?

Conflict

Why do the teen years create so much conflict between you, your parent(s), and your siblings?

During your high school career you, your parents, your teachers, your coaches, and your pastors all have a common goal: to equip you to lead a happy, successful life. Some of those caregivers also hope to mentor you in the Christ-centered life.

So if everyone has the same goal, why all the conflict?

First thing to note: A certain amount of conflict is normal.

> A certain amount of conflict is normal.

A strong-willed puppy on a walk with his owner is one big tug of war. The puppy pulls at his leash because he wants to explore the neighborhood. Most of the time his owner lets the puppy have his own way—at least to the length of the leash.

Sometimes, though, the puppy wants to run into a busy street, explore a bee's nest, sniff poison ivy, bark at a cat, or walk in a yard where a mean dog lives. His owner pulls on the leash, but what does the puppy do? Does he say, "Thank you, master"? No, because he cannot understand why he can't have his own way.

Sometimes when the risk is low the owner may say, "Okay, I'll let you bark at that cat." The owner knows the cat is going to try to scratch out his puppy's eyes, but he also knows there are some things a puppy just has to learn the hard way.

Other risks, like running in a busy street, are simply too great. So the owner restrains the puppy against his will. Some things a puppy can learn through trial and error; other things he must learn by obedience training.

> One of your parents' main tasks is to help you overcome folly and gain wisdom...

Proverbs 22:15 says, "Folly is bound up in the heart of a child, but the rod of discipline will drive it far from him." One of your parents' main parenting tasks is to help you overcome folly and gain wisdom. This requires discipline.

Parents who take this responsibility seriously understand what happens to children who grow up without proper guidance—they often ruin their lives. Proverbs 19:3 puts it like this: "A man's own folly ruins his life, yet his heart rages against the LORD."

A lot of the conflict you will have with your parent(s) is simply a different view of how much leash you should be given in a particular situation. While a puppy's owner may be overprotective, he no doubt has the best interests of the puppy in mind. This is worth remembering.

Q *Do you believe your parents have your best interests in mind, and why or why not?*

Conflict Management

> ... *because they know if you don't, that folly can ruin your life.*

On the other hand, parents are human and they make mistakes. So regular, open, honest communication about your privileges and responsibilities can keep you and your parents "together" on the length of your leash.

Disagreements and conflicts in families are a sure thing. Some families have a stated method for conflict management and talk about disagreements openly. Other families don't have a stated plan, but still do a good job of resolving conflict. Many families don't have a plan, so they don't resolve conflicts with maturity. Without a plan or method, hurt feelings never get dealt with openly, so bitterness and resentment build up.

This is a difficult area for many families. Part of your initiation into manhood is to become a spiritual leader. If you're not sure or don't know how your parents want to handle conflict, be a leader and ask your parents to explain their ideas about how to manage and resolve conflicts.

You could say something like, "Mom/Dad, could we have a family meeting to discuss what's important to you and how we handle it when I mess up? I'd like us to talk about curfew, house rules, calling ahead, not

> *Most successful families have a plan for conflict management.*

calling when I'm late, my use of the car, types of events I go to, who I hang out with, how we determine who gets to sit in the front seat of the car, what is disrespectful, and (whatever else you think important). I'd also like to express my opinions about these issues."

Q *Does your family have a method for dealing constructively with parental and sibling conflict? Is it explicit or implied?*

Do you know how much leash you have been given? Do you think it is too much or not enough? What do you think your parents are trying to accomplish?

Belligerent: Not Pleasant to Be Around

While a certain amount of conflict is normal, as a teen I was way beyond normal.

When I was in the ninth grade I was in the National Honor Society, playing football, and doing pretty well. By the tenth grade I had become a very belligerent young man.

> My parents could do nothing right. They had become the dumbest people on earth.

My parents could say or do nothing right. They had become the dumbest people on earth. When they said, "No," they were the meanest people I had ever met. When I pestered them into changing their "No" to a "Yes" I despised them for being weak.

What I needed most was a good spanking (or at least some very firm discipline). Instead, I kept talking my way into more and more trouble. I lied even when the truth would have worked better. I perfected the fine art of lying.

By the eleventh grade I was skipping school regularly, hanging out at the pool hall, and growing more restless (as well as shiftless) by the day. I could see that I was pretty persuasive and used that ability not only to get what I wanted, but often to get what I didn't really want just because I could.

What *did* I really want? I desperately wanted two things from my parents. First, *I wanted them to believe in me.* I know they tried, but how

> *I had become a very belligerent young man.*

could they when I did not act responsibly? Second, *I wanted them to take me seriously,* but I was not serious.

My daughter is a counselor. She worked with a group of eight parents of teenagers thirteen to eighteen years of age. Someone asked her, "What's the main problem those parents are having?"

She said, "Their teenagers are belligerent. They just will not obey their parents. They won't accept their parents' authority. They are irritable to be around."

Here is the core of the problem: You are in a process of growing up. You are pulling on one end of a leash trying to become independent. Your parent(s) are pulling on the other end. They think they are trying to keep you from harm. You think they are holding you back. It ends up feeling like a tug of war.

Your parent(s) want what's best for you (even if they have a hard time showing it). Normal parents want to give their teenage sons wings, but without pulling up the roots. They want to give you some rope, but not enough to hang yourself. Sometimes you just need to trust their judgment. Other times you just need to be willing to be a man under authority. Honest and open communication is a must.

Dave Matthews sings about how he eventually discovered that parents are for us, not against us. He begins a song,

> It's such a waste, child, to live and die
> for the dreams of our fathers . . .

He ends the song,

> This love I possess I must confess,
> it must be the dreams of our fathers.

Q *How belligerent are you to be around as a son? As a brother?*

What do you really want from your parents? Are you giving them reason to give it to you?

Siblings

The problem with your siblings, if you have any, is that they are pulling on a leash too, but in a different direction. Your brothers and sisters have their own problems and challenges. It is difficult to suggest this because I never did it, but the best thing you can do is to *serve* your brothers and sisters in Christlike humility.

Jesus said, "A new command I give you: Love one another" (John 13:34). Loving and serving your siblings can potentially change the family climate. For example, one young man, Michael, decided to be nice to his older brother. After a while his older brother started offering to drive him places.

Q *What would happen if you served your brothers and sisters? What is the proper motivation to serve them?*

Frequent Questions

How much should I tell my parents about relationships at school and how should I react to what they say? The key to talking with your parents is mutual respect. If they respect you, you will talk to them. If you respect them, they will take you seriously. Your parents have wisdom that can help you. Also, no one loves you or wants the best for you like your parents.

What do I do if I feel rejected by my parents? First, call a special meeting and tell your parent(s) how you feel. Make some written notes in advance of your meeting. Writing things down helps you clarify what you want to say. Also, your notes will help you remember what you want to get across during your meeting.

There's a good chance your parent(s) will be shocked you feel that way and want to make corrections. However, don't get discouraged if they don't see things the same way you do right away. Many people need some time to get used to new ideas. Also, you should be open to additional thoughts from your parents.

And if they don't come around and you still feel rejected? God will protect you. The psalmist wrote, "Even if my father and mother abandon me, the LORD will hold me close" (Psalm 27:10 NLT).

How much time should I spend with my family instead of going out with my friends all the time? It's normal for teenage boys to want to be with their friends. Try to eat breakfast and dinner with your family, or as many family members as possible. You could ride to church together, maybe sit together sometimes. If you watch TV, consider doing that together. Ask your dad to take you to a movie or out to dinner one night a week. If your family does something like bike rides, camping, or goes to college football games, go along sometimes.

A Challenge

God has put parents in charge (meaning, "given them authority") of raising sons and daughters of godly character and faith. Most parents are trying pretty hard to be good moms and dads, including single parents, blended families, and joint-custody families.

Most conflicts are really power struggles over who is in charge. The Bible says, "Children, obey your parents in everything, for this pleases the Lord" (Colossians 3:20). The Bible does not say to obey them only if you agree with them. You need to obey your parents for a lot of reasons, but mostly because that's what Christ wants for you at this age. The only exception would be if you are the subject of abuse.

The more you put yourself under their authority and obey them, the more Christ can move in their hearts to bless you. An important part of your initiation into manhood is obedience as a son.

What are the reasons you should obey your parents? Are there any exceptions?

PART

5 | LIFE SKILLS

11 | becoming independent

Your #1 goal as a teenager is to prepare for a life independent of your parents. Your parents' #1 goal is to equip you for life independent of them.

Everyone agrees on the goal: to equip you to be independent so you can do something with your life. Both you and your parents know this instinctively, even if you've never talked about it in these exact words.

A better way of stating this goal, however, is actually not to gain *independence,* but to *transfer dependence* upon your parents to dependence upon Jesus Christ. An authentic man is not independent—he is dependent upon Christ.

Your parents are agents of Jesus Christ. They have a God-given task—a calling—to protect, train, and equip you for life. So to understand what your parents are doing, you need to understand what God is doing.

The Bible says things like

- We are his masterpiece, created in Christ Jesus to do good things he planned for us long ago (see Ephesians 2:10).
- He (God) who began a good work within you is faithful to complete it (see Philippians 1:6).

> *An authentic man is not independent—he is dependent upon Christ.*

- God is working in you, giving you the desire to obey him and the power to do what pleases him (see Philippians 2:13).
- Let that mind which is in Christ Jesus be in you also (see Philippians 2:5).
- Be transformed by the renewing of your mind (see Romans 12:2).
- You are predestined to be conformed to the image of Christ (see Romans 8:29).

Your parents no doubt want you to have increasing *privileges, duties, rights,* and *responsibilities.* The conflicts you have with your parents are usually not about *whether* you should have increased privileges and responsibilities, but about their *timing.*

When Chad went into the ninth grade his parents sat down with him and said, "These are your increased freedoms. These are your responsibilities. The freedoms and responsibilities go hand in hand. If you abuse either, then we will have to make an appropriate adjustment."

How comfortable do you feel talking with your parents about your privileges, duties, rights, and responsibilities? (If you don't talk about these matters, you are now at an age that would be a good time to start.)

Your Design

Over the next several years your parents will transfer responsibility for your life to you, and you will accept the responsibility. To accomplish this you will need to focus on learning your *design* and your *calling.*

To "do something with your life" is to figure out what you can do well—how God has designed you.

If you are 5 feet 6 inches tall, have an 8-inch vertical leap, are quiet, and like to work with numbers, you are never going to play pro basketball. You may, however, thoroughly enjoy an accounting career.

> *God needs men in every arena who will redeem those arenas for Christ.*

If you love meeting new people, don't like paperwork, and prefer to be outdoors, you may not enjoy accounting. You may, however, thoroughly enjoy a career in sales.

God needs men in every arena—business, transportation, medicine, education, government, law enforcement, the building trades, the legal and justice system, the military, sports, the arts—who will do something with their lives to redeem those arenas for God's glory.

Your Natural Abilities

God has designed you in a special way for a special mission (this is your personal purpose mentioned in chapter 5). He has wired you in a certain way. One of your great pleasures will be to find and fulfill your destiny. To do that, you need to know what you have been designed to do well. Your design consists of both *natural* and *spiritual* abilities.

You are naturally gifted with one or more, usually several, types of natural intelligence. Howard Gardner of Harvard University proposed his widely accepted theory of multiple intelligences in his book *Frames of Mind*.[9] Think about your own life as you review the eight types of intelligence he has identified:

___ Linguistic Intelligence—Sensitivity to meaning and order of words. Language experts, writers, public speakers.

___ Logical-Mathematical Intelligence—Ability in math and complex logical systems. Computer technologists, engineers, scientists.

___ Musical Intelligence—Ability to understand and create music. Musicians, composers, dancers.

___ Spatial Intelligence—Ability to perceive visual world accurately and re-create or alter it mentally or on paper. Designers, architects, air traffic controllers.

___ Bodily-Kinesthetic Intelligence—Ability to use the body in skilled way to express self, attain goals, or entertainment. Athletes, dancers, actors.

___ Interpersonal Intelligence—Ability to perceive and understand other individuals' moods, desires, and motivations. Business leaders, politicians, teachers, therapists.

___ Intrapersonal Intelligence—Ability to understand personal emotions, values, and philosophy. Contemplative writers, counselors, inventors, religious leaders.

___ Naturalist Intelligence—Sensitive to nature and perceives connections, patterns, and distinctions in the natural world. Biologists, naturalists, environmentalists, foresters, agronomists.[10]

You may find it helpful to take a moment and evaluate yourself. In the blank spaces above, put a "1" by the intelligence with which you most identify, a "2" by your second highest, and a "3" by your third highest.

Exploring and developing your natural intelligence will empower you to lead a more full, abundant life for God's glory—independent of your parents and dependent upon Christ. They are "pointers."

Q *Why do you think it would be helpful to explore this?*
Which types of intelligence do you know you have for sure? To which are you drawn?
Which types of intelligence would you like to explore and develop?

Your Spiritual Gifts

Biblically, you will also have one or more spiritual gifts. Spiritual gifts are special spiritual abilities that equip you to do something with your life. They can be used in both the church and the world for God's glory.

> *Every believer receives at least one spiritual gift.*

Every believer receives at least one spiritual gift. "Now to each one the manifestation of the Spirit is given for the common good" (1 Corinthians 12:7). The Holy Spirit determines our spiritual gifts. "He gives them to each one, just as he determines" (1 Corinthians 12:11).

The purpose of our spiritual gifts is to serve Christ by serving others, helping to fulfill the Great Commission (God's plan to help people become Christians and grow) and the Cultural Mandate (God's plan to tend the world). If you want to look them up, there are four passages of Scripture that discuss spiritual gifts—Romans 12:4–8; 1 Corinthians 12:4–11, 28–31; Ephesians 4:11–13; and 1 Peter 4:10–11.

Spiritual gifts include *service* gifts, *speaking* gifts, and *signifying* gifts. While theologians and teachers differ somewhat on how to classify and name these gifts, the following generally captures the gist of the various gifts.[11]

NOTE: *You may find it helpful to mark any gifts you know (or suspect) you have in the blank spaces provided.*

Service Gifts

Service gifts are often low-profile, behind-the-scene gifts. Here are brief definitions of the service gifts with a few examples of how each gift may be used:

___ *Mercy:* Special ability to show sympathy to those who are suffering. Calling students who are sick, hospital visits, phone calls and visits to the hurting or to nursing homes.

___ *Service:* Special ability to joyfully serve behind the scenes. Set up chairs, make phone calls, assist leaders.

___ *Hospitality:* Special desire to offer home, food, and lodging. Host exchange students, Bible studies, new friends to dinner or your lunch group.

___ *Giving:* Special desire and financial ability to give above and beyond a tithe. Generosity toward youth mission trips, the poor, evangelistic ministries.

___ *Administration:* Special ability to orchestrate program details. Committee work, volunteer to organize youth group activities, conference/seminar/retreat supervision.

___ *Leadership:* Special ability to preside or govern wisely. Leadership team of youth group, chair school committees, school club officer, visible leadership roles.

___ *Faith:* Vision for new projects that need doing and perseverance to see them through. Start new ministries at school, start prayer club, help plan youth group mission trip.

___ *Discernment:* Ability to detect error. Meet with teachers who may be teaching incorrectly, write letters to the editor.

Speaking Gifts

"If anyone speaks, he should do it as one speaking the very words of God" (1 Peter 4:11). People who have been given speaking gifts are able to help equip others to have a personal ministry of service. Here are definitions and examples of the speaking gifts:

___ *Knowledge:* Spiritual ability to search and acquire scriptural truth. Academic pursuits, writing, teaching.

___ *Wisdom:* Special insight into applications of knowledge. Counseling, teaching, discussion group leader, accountability groups, friendship.

___ *Preaching:* Special ability to rightly proclaim and expound God's truth. Preachers, lay preachers.

___ *Teaching:* Special ability to explain Scripture in edifying way. Sunday school teachers, Bible studies, home groups, children, youth programs.

___ *Evangelism:* Special ability to clearly present the gospel to non-believers. Youth group visitors, share faith at school, sponsor student outreach events.

___ *Apostleship:* Special ability to begin new works. Missionaries, church planters, Christian service organizations.

___ *Shepherding:* Unique ability to care for a flock of believers over the long haul. Pastors, elders, assist youth pastor, work in nursery program.

___ *Encouragement:* Special skill to inspire, encourage, and comfort. Being a friend, counseling, writing letters.

Signifying Gifts

The signifying gifts are miracles, healing, speaking in tongues, and the interpretation of tongues. Different denominations have different views about the current presence and use of these gifts. Check with your parents and/or pastors.

___ *Tongues:* Spiritual ability to speak in a language foreign to speaker.

___ *Interpretation of Tongues:* Spiritual ability to interpret the message of one speaking in tongues.

___ *Miracles:* Spiritual ability to bring about the supernatural intervention of God against the laws of nature.

___ *Healing:* Spiritual agency of God in curing illness and disease and restoring to health supernaturally.

Which spiritual gifts are you pretty sure you have? Which ones do you suspect you may have?

Your Calling

In addition to settling the issues of *identity*—"who you are" and *purpose*—"why you exist" (discussed in chapters 4 and 5), in the years

> *A calling is that vocation you can give yourself to without reservation that creates a passionate desire for excellence, to be your best.*

ahead you will also settle the important question of *calling*—"what you will do."

The calling of a student is different than the calling of an adult. Your calling as a student is to prepare yourself for taking on the roles of manhood.

It would be pretty unusual for you to already have a sense of God's calling on your adult life. I mention that now so you don't think you have to know your calling at this point in your life. But it is important for you to know about the biblical concept of calling, or vocation.

What is a man's "calling"? Here's a good working definition: *A calling is that vocation you can give yourself to without reservation that creates a passionate desire for excellence, to be your best.* It is the thing you are "able" to do because of interest, natural abilities (Gardner's intelligences), and spiritual gifts.

This calling will be how you "tend the culture." It can be as formal as a job or as informal as "what you do during the day." It is probably not as tightly defined as a specific job description you do or a company you work for (like pharmaceutical salesperson), but the "type" of work you can give yourself to with enthusiasm (like persuading people to purchase useful products).

Examples of callings could include software design, plumbing, management, engineering, or the practice of law. Or, you may choose to describe your calling at the level of your "life's work" and remain more general, like "solving problems" rather than management, or "designing things" instead of engineering.

A calling includes what you do, but it is more. It is something you can give yourself to for the betterment of mankind, which at the same time brings you joy and fulfillment. It is the vocation that kindles fresh fire each new morning. A calling is not merely a means to other ends (though it will be); a calling is an end in itself.

Q *What hints do you have so far (interests, intelligences, gifts) about what your vocational calling might be?*

A Challenge

As you prepare for a life independent of your parents, your best success will come from understanding your design—how God has wired you.

Your parents, mentors, and I can "ask you up" into manhood, but to maximize your manhood you're going to need to understand the equipment God has given you. Why not take some time with a pencil and mark your natural abilities and spiritual gifts in the spaces provided in this chapter.

Ask yourself, "Is there any vocation I could give myself to unreservedly that creates in me a passionate desire for excellence, to be my best?" It's not likely this will already be obvious to you, but maybe. Your natural abilities and spiritual gifts will offer you interesting clues about your eventual calling.

> *A calling includes what you do, but it is more.*

12 | how to make important decisions

Ben was a school leader, a solid "B" student, a respected member of the football team, and he felt invincible.

One morning at 4:00 A.M. Ben crawled out his window, "borrowed" his mom's Mercedes, picked up three other boys, and went for a joy ride. They were not drinking. They came to a long, straight stretch on a two-lane highway with no other cars in sight.

Ben made a split-second decision to see how fast the car would go. He punched his foot to the floor and the car leaped forward to 80, then 90, 100, 110, 120, and finally 130 miles per hour. Not wanting to appear uncool, the other boys didn't protest, but double-checked their seat belts. Ben's belt was not fastened.

As the car hit 130 mph, a curve seemed to appear out of nowhere. Ben tried to slow down and turn the car, but the entry speed into the corner exceeded 100 mph. The centrifugal force popped all four tires off the rims. The car skidded through the curves on the rims, off the road, then flipped through the air several times. When the car finally came to rest, remarkably, Ben's three passengers were shaken but not seriously hurt.

Ben, on the other hand, had been thrown from the car and sustained critical injuries. In the days ahead the doctors were able to patch Ben back together again. However, a sizeable piece of his skull had to be removed. His brain was damaged. The recovery was long.

Months later Ben stood beside the football field and watched his buddies practice. Ben would never play sports again. His hopes for a scholarship had vanished. His biggest challenge became learning how to speak again.

Q *Can you see yourself doing something like what Ben did, and why or why not?*

The Power of Choice

> We have been given an incredible gift: the power of choice.

We have each been given an incredible gift: the power of choice or, if you prefer, free will. As illustrated in Ben's story, we make real choices that have real consequences.

Some choices, of course, are small stuff— what to wear today, work out after school or skip it, go out or stay home. The consequences of those choices don't make much difference. Other choices have major consequences.

The purpose of this book is to help initiate you into manhood. Few things are more important to manhood than making wise choices.

> We make real choices that have real consequences.

The focus in this chapter is, "How do you make major decisions wisely?" There are decisions that, once made, alter our lives—whether made in a split second, after many months of weighing options, or as the result of many (seemingly) smaller choices that just sort of add up over time. Examples of major decisions include:

- to live in peace or conflict with your parents
- which group of friends to hang with
- whether or not to embrace Christ
- whether or not to live openly for God

- whether or not to wait until marriage for sex
- whether or not to experiment with smoking, drugs, or alcohol
- whether or not to go to college
- and, later, decisions about where to go to college, what you will major in, what career field you pursue, which woman you marry, what city you live in, and so on.

> *There are two kinds of decisions: moral and priority.*

There are two kinds of decisions in life: *moral* and *priority.* A moral decision is a choice between *right* and *wrong.* There is a definite right thing to do and a definite wrong thing to do. For example, should you let someone copy your homework when they're not supposed to? Do you withhold your friendship from someone merely because of his ethnicity?

A priority decision is a choice between *right* and *right.* In other words, there are no moral implications of either choice. For example, do you go to junior college or state? Do you work after school or play sports? Do you play soccer and basketball, or just soccer? Do you date or kiss dating goodbye? These are priority choices, not moral choices. There is no one right answer.

In this chapter I want to give you the principles for making wise major decisions—whether moral or priority.

Think of a major decision you recently made. Was it a moral or priority decision? Was it difficult and, if so, why? How did you handle it?

> *A moral decision is a choice between right and wrong.*

Three Principles of Decision Making

The goal of any decision is to be wise. Proverbs 3:13–18 says:

Blessed is the man who finds wisdom, the man who
gains understanding, for she is more profitable than silver
and yields better returns than gold. She is more precious
than rubies; nothing you desire can compare with her.
Long life is in her right hand; in her left hand are riches
and honor. Her ways are pleasant ways, and all her paths
are peace. She is a tree of life to those who embrace her;
those who lay hold of her will be blessed.

> *A priority decision is a choice between two rights.*

Let's look at three principles of making major decisions with wisdom.

1. *Realize that many major decisions do turn out wrong.* We see this in Ben's story. Obviously, crawling out his window at 4:00 A.M. and driving 130 mph were terrible decisions.

2. *Count the cost of making the wrong decision.* The decision to cheat on an exam is a lot different than not studying for the test. To not study for a test is a "one day" consequence. To cheat may signal a "lifetime" issue. What will happen if you buy a used car, don't get a mechanic to check out the engine and drivetrain, and the car turns out to be a lemon? It will hurt, but you're not going to die. But suppose the car you buy is a really fast Mustang, so you want to see what it's got. You challenge a Vette at a traffic light. You could end up like Ben. Probably not, but it is worth counting the cost of being wrong.

3. *Most decisions are obvious given enough information and time.* You can't decide whether to play soccer or not. You can't decide whether to work after school to save money for a car. You can't decide what college to attend.

When do we make poor decisions? When we don't have our facts straight, or when we are hasty. Here is a sentence worth memorizing: *It is easy to look at the data and come to the wrong conclusion.*

Keep collecting data. Write it down so you don't forget it. The mind by itself may blow one small fact out of proportion. Writing things down puts them in perspective. It's a lot better to operate from fact than feeling.

Q *Do you think you have been mostly wise in your past decisions, and why or why not?*

The Means to Find God's Will

Most of the major decisions we make in life are not dictated by Scripture. So what do we do?

We will make better major decisions if we abide in Christ daily, begin each day in humble surrender to God, seek to please him in all our ways, and live our lives out of the overflow of our personal relationship with Jesus. To assist us, God has given us means of guidance. Let's briefly explore each of seven different means God has given us to help discern his will.

1. The Bible. The single most important question to ask is, "Has God already spoken on this matter?" The Bible is chock-full of commands (which are duty) and principles (which are wise). We don't have to wonder if we should be kind to a goofy kid. The Bible has already covered it. Obedience is the trademark of a biblical Christian. Talk about the Scriptures with your peers. As the Bible says, "Do not go beyond what is written" (1 Corinthians 4:6).

2. Prayer. Jesus said, "Until now you have not asked for anything in my name. Ask and you will receive, and your joy will be complete" (John 16:24). Over and over and over again we are invited to present our requests to God. Prayer is the currency of our personal relationship with Christ. Spend it liberally. Pray over major (why not all?) decisions.

3. *The Holy Spirit.* God lives in us in the person of the Holy Spirit. He is our counselor, convicter, comforter, converter, and encourager. Consciously depend upon him, and he will both guide you and intercede for you. "The Spirit intercedes for the saints in accordance with God's will" (Romans 8:27). The Holy Spirit is the one who gives us the wisdom and power to make good decisions. The Holy Spirit will never lead you in a way that contradicts his written Word.

4. *Conscience.* In seeking God's will we must live in good conscience toward God and other people. "Dear friends, if our hearts do not condemn us, we have confidence before God" (1 John 3:21). Keep in mind that while a guilty conscience provides clear evidence you are not in God's will, a clear conscience may not guarantee you have correctly discerned God's will. Conscience is more effective as a red light than a green light. To go against conscience is neither wise nor safe.

5. *Circumstances.* Some people are born short, some tall. Some black, some white. Some in America, some in Argentina. Some to poor parents, some to rich. God's will is often revealed clearly by the circumstances in which we live. "He determined the times set for them and the exact places where they should live" (Acts 17:26). If you want a motorcycle but your parents have adamantly said, "No," then circumstances have told you God's will. If you want to take up wakeboarding but don't live on a lake, don't have a boat, and don't know anyone who does, your circumstances are telling you God's will about the matter.

6. *Counsel.* "Plans fail for lack of counsel, but with many advisers they succeed" (Proverbs 15:22). Often we need nothing more than a good listener to help us crystallize our thoughts into coherent words. Other times, we need the advice of a trusted friend. Seek out people you trust and get their advice. Seek the counsel of people who have a track

record for making wise decisions. Get other people's perspectives. Talk to experts in the area, like a guidance counselor or youth pastor. Consult your parents. Choose your friends carefully (or at least the ones you listen to) because, as the Bible says, "Bad company corrupts good character" (1 Corinthians 15:33).

7. *Fasting.* Fasting is an often overlooked spiritual activity. Fasting slows down the physical functions so that the mind can be more in tune with Christ. Fasting demonstrates a seriousness about your concern to the Lord. I mention it here because it's biblical, and I can personally recommend it.[12]

If you regularly use these means for finding the will of God, I believe you will achieve the wisdom you are seeking for the major decisions you must make.

Q *Which of these seven means of guidance would you most like to have more of, and why?*

A Process to Find God's Will

Here is a useful, practical process for finding the will of God. Keep in mind this is not a process for getting our own way. We must be cautious that we truly want what God wants. Otherwise we will twist things to our own way. Each step builds on itself, and you may find the answer becomes obvious at any point along the way. If the right answer doesn't make itself clear, keep moving through the steps until it does.

1. *Write down the decision exactly.* Nothing clarifies our thinking more quickly than paper and pencil. It's said that half the solution is correctly knowing the problem. Francis Bacon said, "Writing maketh an exact man." Precisely what is the decision? What are the options?

Example: "Should I continue to resist the temptation to try drugs?"

Example: _____.

2. Next, write out a "purpose statement" that precisely explains why you are considering this decision. It is helpful not only to know what you are trying to decide, but why. "Why" are you trying to decide "what" you are trying to decide? What is the context? Is it a need or a want? Are you unhappy?

Example: "I am trying to decide whether to continue resisting the temptation to try drugs because most of my friends have tried them. They say it's fun, nobody I know has been hurt by it, and I don't want to be left out."

Example: _____.

3. *Next, submit your purpose statement to a series of questions.* Here are some suggestions:

- What are you trying to accomplish, and why?
  Example: "To not feel left out."
  Example: _____.

- What is your objective, or desired end result?
  Example: "To keep a godly witness to my friends."
  Example: _____.

- What are your expectations and why?
  Example: "If I don't, my friends may drop me."
  Example: _____.

- How does this decision fit in with your calling?
  Example: "If I use drugs, I will violate my own beliefs."
  Example: _____.

- What would Jesus do if he were you? What is the "next" right step to take?
  Example: "He would not take them. I should challenge my friends to do right."
  Example: _____.

4. If your answer still hasn't become obvious, list each option on a separate sheet of paper. On the left side, list the advantages of that option; on the right side, list the disadvantages. As Professor Louis Agazziz said, "A pencil is one of the best of eyes." Usually, one option will prove itself clearly desirable, or undesirable, at this point.

5. At all times, employ the seven steps of guidance to discern God's will (covered on pages 101–103).

6. If the answer still hasn't come, wait. You can never predict what God is doing in your life. God is not a man, and he would never work for your harm. God is committed to working for your good. Commit to let God set the agenda. Never push God. If the answer isn't obvious, trust him to make it clear in his timing. You can rush ahead, but you do so at your own peril. Better to wait upon the Lord. Give him the time he wants to work some things into and out of your character. And remember this: God is not the author of confusion. Satan, however, is. If you are still confused, wait. Peace is the umpire.

Q Fill in the "Example" blanks above for a major decision you are trying to make right now.

A Challenge

The man you become will, in large part, be defined by the choices you make over the next few years. Why not decide right now that to the best of your ability you will always seek God's will for your life in every choice. Here is a suggested prayer to express your desire:

Lord, I will do anything you want me to do. Help me to always seek your plan, purpose, and will in every decision. Help me to remember that it is easy to look at the data and come to the wrong conclusion. Help me to have no agenda but you, and no agenda but yours. Transform and renew my mind so that I may know—and do—your good, pleasing, and perfect will in every situation. In Jesus' name, Amen.

You won't be perfect in this, but it will give you a reference point. Let me encourage you to keep this chapter in mind. Review it when you seem to get stuck on a major decision.

CHAPTER
13 | integrity and other values

The clerk at Starbucks rang up $1.50 for my $3.50 cafe mocha. When I told him he had made a mistake he said, "It's okay. Don't worry about it."

I said, "No, really, I would rather pay the right price."

He said, "Don't worry about it. It's on me." What he really meant, of course, was that he was going to let his company absorb the loss.

A friend and I went to the movies. He qualifies for the senior discount. He purchased his ticket first and said, "One senior, please."

Then I put down my money and said, "One, please." When the clerk gave me change, I realized he had rung me up at the discount price.

When I brought this to his attention he said, "That's okay. Don't worry about it."

I said, "No, I want to pay the regular price."

He said, "No, really, it's okay."

I said, "No, it's not. I need to pay the right price." I could tell by the puzzled look on his face that this didn't compute for him. By now, the line behind me was becoming impatient.

> *"If you have integrity, nothing else matters. If you don't have integrity, nothing else matters."*
> *—former U.S. Senator Alan Simpson*

He said, "Sir, really, it's no big deal." He just didn't get it. I walked away, shaking my head.

One day I bought a Philly cheese steak and a coke, but the girl at the register only charged me for the sandwich. I brought this to her attention and she said, "Don't worry about it. It's on the house." At least she was clear-headed enough not to say, "It's on me." I couldn't get her to understand it was wrong. I tried—I really did.

Q *Have you had an experience like one of these? If so, what happened?*

Should We Be Worried?

Don't worry about it? Should we? Jesus said something very interesting about this topic of integrity: "Whoever can be trusted with very little can also be trusted with much, and whoever is dishonest with very little will also be dishonest with much. So if you have not been trustworthy in handling worldly wealth, who will trust you with true riches? And if you have not been trustworthy with someone else's property, who will give you property of your own?" (Luke 16:10–12).

> *If you have not been trustworthy in handling worldly wealth, who will trust you with true riches?*

I don't know how you feel about it, but I have too many big things I would like to see God do in my life to risk blowing it over little fudges here and there. Besides, I'm old enough to know that even a small compromise now will always and inevitably lead to bigger lapses later.

There is another, greater reason for having integrity. St. Augustine once said, "Love God, and do what you want." What he meant was that if we really, truly, and deeply love God, then we will be prone to choose the right thing in every situation. Of course, none of us will ever do this perfectly—it's a guiding principle, not just another rule we won't be able to keep.

So integrity is a way of expressing our faith in, and love for, Christ. Let's take a look at what integrity means.

Q *What strikes you personally about what Jesus said in the passage above?*

> "Love God, and do what you want."
>
> —St. Augustine

Integrity Defined

Perhaps no other word describes the inward *character* and outward *conduct* of an authentic man as well as the word *integrity*. *Merriam-Webster's Collegiate Dictionary* reads

integrity *noun*

1: firm adherence to a code of especially moral or artistic values: INCORRUPTIBILITY

2: an unimpaired condition: SOUNDNESS

3: the quality or state of being complete or undivided: COMPLETENESS

What does it mean to be a man of integrity? Integrity means living by your code. Integrity means being undivided—a man of integrity doesn't waver between two opinions. He doesn't fold under pressure. Other men under pressure may make mistakes, but pressure only makes a man of integrity more determined to do the right thing.

A man of integrity stands his ground. He is not double-minded or easily swayed. His loyalties are not split. He cannot be corrupted. He has decided in advance to hold his position, no matter what the cost. He takes personal responsibility for his inward character and outward conduct, while trusting Christ to empower him through the Holy Spirit. The Marines come to mind, as do several young men who participated in a pilot study group for this book. Incorruptible, sound, complete. Not flawless, but determined in Christ.

> Integrity means living by your code. A man of integrity stands his ground.

The Bible gives a good picture of integrity when some religious leaders described Jesus: "They came to him and said, 'Teacher, we know you are a man of integrity. You aren't swayed by men, because you pay no attention to who they are; but you teach the way of God in accordance with the truth'" (Mark 12:13).

Notice that Jesus

- was not swayed by men,
- would not pay attention to a man just because of his position,
- taught (and lived) God's way, and
- lived according to the truth.

Here's a core concept you can memorize that will help you walk as a man of integrity:

> ### *Integrity is a one-to-one correlation between my Bible, my beliefs, and my behavior.*

Let's unpack this idea. Let's start with behavior and work backward. For our lives to have authentic Christian integrity, there must be a one-to-one correlation between our *behavior* and our *beliefs*. They have to "match up." For example, if I "say" I love my neighbor, but I am not willing to listen to him when he is hurting, I lack a correlation between my behavior and belief—I don't have integrity.

And to have authentic Christian integrity there must be a one-to-one correlation between our *beliefs* and our *Bibles*. For example, if I "believe" that sex before marriage is no big deal, and my Bible says it is a big deal, I lack a correlation between my belief and my Bible.

Q *Which of the ways to describe integrity just mentioned "connects" for you, and why?*

Integrity vs. Judgment

One day I was pulling up to a stop sign talking on my cell phone. I didn't come to a full stop. Technically, I broke the law. Was that an integrity problem? Can you break a law and not be dishonest?

Another day I was backed up for two blocks waiting to get through a traffic light. My car was stopped at an intersection with a side street. Someone pulled up to the side street stop sign and looked over to me to see if I would let him in. What he didn't know was that I was incredibly late for an appointment and totally stressed out. Although I always let people in, this time I didn't. I felt guilty as I eased by. Was this an integrity problem?

There are many choices we make that are *errors in judgment* but not *lapses of integrity.* You may still have to pay the consequence. For example, if a policeman sees you accidentally run a stop sign you will get a ticket—especially if he sees you talking on your cell phone. But the Bible makes a distinction between an *intentional* and *unintentional* sin (Numbers 15:22–30).

Q *What is the difference between an integrity problem and an error in judgment?*
Is a sin only a sin if you get caught?

How We Get Integrity

One of your teachers gives you a homework assignment that has to be turned in and counts toward your grade. Chase approaches you before class on the due date and says, "Hey, man. I had a really bad night last night. My girlfriend and I had a fight. We were on the phone until after midnight. It was tough, really tough. Can you help me out and let me copy your homework? I would really appreciate it—I really would." What do you do?

You and your girlfriend find yourself alone at her house one afternoon after school. She is love-starved and vulnerable. She puts her hand on your thigh. You know that she wants to have sex with you. All you have to do is make the move. You don't even have to ask. What do you do?

Your mom is waiting for you when you get home—an hour after curfew. You know your mom thinks you are the greatest. You know that if you tell her that it was your friends' fault she will let you off. But the truth is that you made no effort to get home on time. What do you do?

How do we get integrity? A lot of it comes from family values—probably most of it if your family's values are good. We also pick it up by "watching" people we respect—by seeing how they handle dicey situations. We get integrity from reading God's Word—the Bible. We get it from an inward commitment to live our lives before Jesus with authenticity. We get it by depending upon Jesus to give us the strength to be a man, a real man.

Q *How would you handle each of the three situations in this section with integrity?*

Once and for Always

In my daughter's dorm at college the laundry room's washers and dryers took quarters. The girls figured out they could put two quarters inside a pair of nylon stockings, insert the quarters in the slots, push in the lever, start the machine, then pull the lever out and retrieve their quarters.

> It will always cost you more to be honest.

My daughter, frustrated because she didn't have much money, said half-seriously, "Maybe I should start doing that too." My wife said something that you may as well come to grips with now. She said, "Jen, you will have many choices like this in life, and it will always cost you more to be honest."

It will cost you something to be a man of integrity.

Joseph was horribly mistreated but found favor with God who gave him unusual success. Joseph's master put him in charge of everything he owned. But his master's wife kept coming on to him. The Bible says:

> "The man of integrity walks securely, but he who takes crooked paths will be found out" (Proverbs 10:9).

> Now Joseph was well-built and handsome, and after a while his master's wife took notice of Joseph and said, "Come to bed with me!" But he refused. "With me in charge," he told her, "my master does not concern himself with anything in the house; everything he owns he has entrusted to my care. No one is greater in this house than I am. My master has withheld nothing from me except you, because you are his wife. How then could I do such a wicked thing and sin against God?" And though she spoke to Joseph day after day, he refused to go to bed with her or even be with her (Genesis 39:6–10).

This was a defining moment for Joseph. Joseph made the decision to be a man of integrity. Joseph had decided in advance that he would rather have God's blessing than the momentary pleasures that could come from compromising his integrity.

Other men of the Bible have clung to their integrity:

> David said, "May integrity and uprightness protect me, because my hope is in you" (Psalm 25:21).

The LORD said to Satan, "Have you considered my servant Job? There is no one on earth like him; he is blameless and upright, a man who fears God and shuns evil. And he still maintains his integrity, though you incited me against him to ruin him without any reason" (Job 2:3).

Job said, "I will not deny my integrity" (Job 27:5).

Solomon said, "The integrity of the upright guides them, but the unfaithful are destroyed by their duplicity" (Proverbs 11:3).

Nehemiah said, "I put in charge of Jerusalem my brother Hanani, along with Hananiah the commander of the citadel, because he was a man of integrity and feared God more than most men do" (Nehemiah 7:2).

Has your integrity been confronted with a defining moment? If so, describe it, and what you did. What could it cost you to be a man of integrity? Are you prepared to make a once-for-all decision to be a man of integrity by faith?

Other Values

Integrity is the "core" value of an authentic Christian man, but you will, of course, have other values too. Notice these examples:

- Diligence
- Team player
- Hard worker
- Perseverance
- Courage
- Treats other well

- Patriotism
- Family closeness
- Excellence

Young men (and women) reflect the values of their families—for better or worse. To live differently (not just "better," but for Christ) means to be grateful for parents who have good values, or to ask Christ to change you if you come from a family that didn't stress good values.

Our values are the bedrock upon which we build our lives. Values "inform" every decision we make. They are part of the philosophy of our lives. Together our values form our "system" or worldview. They affect how we see the world, and how we react to it. They are imprinted on our souls. They become part of the fabric of who we are. We don't have to rehearse them before we make a choice—they are always there. They are buried in our gut. Values are our most deeply held beliefs. For the authentic Christian man, values reflect what we believe to be good, right, noble, and true. Our values are an extension of our true identity.

What are some additional examples of values?
What are your three most important values?

A Challenge

It would be easy to make up a list of values and think that if we live up to them, we will become "good," "good enough," or "righteous" in God's sight.

This is the exact opposite of Christ's gospel. There is only one man who has lived a perfectly righteous life—and his name is Jesus. The gospel of Jesus is that we can never "do" anything to make us "good" enough for God to love us. We

> *It would be easy to make up a list of values and think that if we live up to them, we will become "good," "good enough," or "righteous" in God's sight.*

> We are not made righteous by what we do, but through repentance and putting faith in Jesus.

are not made righteous by what we do, but through repentance and putting faith in Jesus. He will never love you more, or less, based upon how righteously you live (your integrity). Instead, God loves you because of Jesus.

When we live by faith, Jesus forms his life in us through his Holy Spirit. He progressively changes our desires so that we want to be men of integrity. But never think we must first become men of integrity to be good enough for God. And never think you will attain it perfectly in this life. Rather, integrity is a response to the good news that Jesus loves and forgives us, not something we do to "merit" his love and forgiveness.

So, one thing we should not do: Don't merely make up a list of values and think that by pursuing them you can become a good or righteous man (this is often called "works righteousness").

This does not, however, mean you shouldn't have a list of values to which you aspire. When you see a peer or mentor living out a value you would like for yourself—say, treating others well, courage, or perseverance—ask Jesus to work it into your character in faith. At the same time, pursue it diligently. God works best as we also put forth cooperative effort.

Q *Do you think you correctly understand Christ's gospel? Explain the difference between a "works righteousness" and a "righteousness that comes by faith."*

How committed are you to being a man of integrity?

14 your secret thought life

Michael, Cameron, David, Collin, Spencer, Hace, and Braden stood around before class trying to guess what questions Mrs. Moore would ask on the English test they were about to take.

Brittany Temple, a senior, came around the corner and briskly walked by these seven underclassmen. Brittany was the most beautiful girl any of them had ever seen—everyone in the whole school knew she was the prettiest girl alive.

As she passed by, her sweater brushed against Michael's arm. He almost fainted.

The scent of her perfume arrived about two seconds later. All seven boys felt dizzy.

Several of them stared at the curvaceous beauty of her shapely figure as she walked away. She could easily have posed for the statue of a Greek goddess!

Overwhelming thoughts of lust and sexual fantasy sprang into action in everyone's minds—thoughts that they worked hard to disguise were happening.

Brittany stopped at her locker for a minute, and their conversation became very stilted. Abruptly, the thirst for knowledge was overwhelmed by the hunger for love. It was Brittany versus Mrs. Moore. The testosterone won, and

> *The scent of her perfume made them dizzy.*

suddenly none of the boys cared very much about what Mrs. Moore might ask on her test.

Spencer and Cameron thought they must be in love. Spencer's chest tightened, his breathing labored, and blood rushed to his head. Brittany was the girl of his dreams.

No sooner had Brittany passed from sight than Nathan Steele rounded the corner. Nathan Steele was in a class of his own, peerless. He was the smartest, most athletic, best looking guy on campus. Everyone knew it—both his admirers and those who hated him for it.

He honored them when he said, "Hey guys, what's up?" as he walked by without breaking stride.

He was the coolest guy around, and he knew it. He always got what he wanted, but Hace and Michael saw through him. What they couldn't understand was how David and Collin could be so taken in. Why couldn't they see how shallow this guy was?

For their part, David and Collin couldn't understand why Hace and Michael were so jealous of Nathan. They thought Nathan was the complete package, the guy who most had it all together. After all, they wondered, wouldn't everyone want to be like Nathan if they could?

As they each were thinking their very different thoughts, Chase walked up to their circle and said, "Hi, guys, ready for the test?"

Chase had to be one of the ten nerdiest guys to ever walk the face of the planet. He made Austin Powers look normal. And he always asked questions that, if you answered honestly, would make you feel either stupid or irresponsible, or both.

Braden couldn't help thinking, *This guy is such a goofball. I wish he would just disappear. I wish we could sell him to a passing caravan of camels on their way to Egypt. I sure hope Brittany doesn't see us talking to Mr. Geek.*

They all tried to ignore him. What they couldn't see was that they had become a clique, excluding people from their group on worldly terms.

Steve DeWitt, also in Mrs. Moore's class, walked up and offered everyone a cigarette. Steve always had an angle. He always had a *Playboy* or *Hustler* magazine he wanted to show all the guys. Sometimes he offered a swig from a flask. One day he tried to coax Spencer and Braden to take a drag off his joint.

All the worldliness of Steve's exploits stuck in everyone's minds: the naked pictures, the feeling the booze gave, the feeling of power and independence that came from taking a drag of Steve's marijuana, and the feeling of acceptance that came from smoking a cigarette.

Q *What part of this story do you relate to most, and why? What kind of person brings out the best in you? What kind of person brings out the worst in you?*

The Problem

How embarrassed would you be if your friends knew what you were really thinking most of the time? If a lot, you're not alone.

We each lead a secret thought life that is very different from the "visible you"—the "you" others know. Often, we are not really in touch with—much less in control of—this secret thought life.

Yet this is part of the "real you"—the "you" known by God. The Bible teaches that God knows every thought we have (Psalm 139:1–2).

Every man, to different degrees, wrestles with secret thoughts of pride, lust, fantasy, envy, anger, bitterness, jealousy, self-doubt, unbelief, and more.

Most young men say they struggle with pride.

No doubt lust and sexual fantasy loom large in your thought life. In his book *Bringing Up Boys,* child psychologist James Dobson notes, "The sex drive in boys is at its lifetime peak between the ages of 16 and 18."[13]

Like most of the young men I've been talking to and meeting with, you probably find that you struggle with pride.

One student said, "Pride is so hard for me. It is the only sin I really can't control. Is it possible to not be so prideful, or get it off my mind?"

Another student said, "I have a problem with a teacher. I know you don't want the details, but my pride gets in the way all the time. What should I do?"

Pride is a core issue. Christian writer C. S. Lewis calls it "The Great Sin." He said: "There is one vice of which no man in the world is free; which every one in the world loathes when he sees it in someone else; and of which hardly any people, except Christians, ever imagine that they are guilty themselves. . . . There is no fault which makes a man more unpopular, and no fault which we are more unconscious of in ourselves. And the more we have it ourselves, the more we dislike it in others. . . . It was through Pride that the devil became the devil."[14]

Your secret thought life may be an ongoing battle to find a sense of personal worth—you don't feel affirmed and valuable as an image of God.

Perhaps in your secret thoughts you realize you're constructing a bitter world of envy and jealousy that is making you into an angry young man—and no one has any idea of the venomous thoughts you feel.

It is not unusual for a man to be bombarded by a steady stream of negative and sinful thoughts.

It is not unusual for a man to have a steady stream of negative and sinful thoughts bombarding his mind. Sometimes it can feel like the devil is dropping laser-guided bombs to find secret chambers in our heads.

Q *"It is not unusual for a man to have a steady stream of negative and sinful thoughts bombarding his mind."*
Is this a comfort and, if so, why?
How much different is the "visible you" from the "real you" based upon your secret thoughts?

The Battle for Your Mind

All men have secret thoughts.

Why do we have secret thoughts, and where do they come from? In the unseen world a spiritual battle of cosmic proportions is taking place to win your mind. I realize how difficult this is to visualize.

Picture your mind as a hill that two armies are trying to control. Whichever army makes it to the top is in the best position to fight off the other army when it tries to capture the hill.

The enemy army is the world, the flesh, and the devil.

The devil is a fallen angel, a real spiritual being bent on evil. He incites men to do wicked and sinful things. The devil wants to capture your mind so you will do mean, wicked, and sinful things—not just big things that destroy (though he will if he can), but also small things that cripple love, trust, and faith.

The Devil's Attack from the Outside

The devil uses the world to attack you from the outside. Satan perverts the good things God created to stimulate secret thoughts of lust, pride, and fantasy. He inspires seedy songs, morally bankrupt movies, and sex-saturated television shows. God inspires the good ones.

One day when my son, John, was a senior in high school, someone returned the Snoop Dogg

> *Satan perverts the good things God created to stimulate secret thoughts of lust, pride, and fantasy.*

CD they had borrowed from him a couple of years earlier. He popped it into his car player a couple of times.

A few days later he ejected the CD, rolled down the window, and tossed it out like a Frisbee. When he told me what he had done I asked, "Why did you do that?"

He said, "Dad, I have a very strong Christian worldview. I am able to distinguish between what's right and wrong without getting confused. But the lyrics on that CD have a lot of cuss words. I found they were getting 'stuck' in my mind. So I decided to get rid of it."

He saw that the world was confusing him, so he rejected the world. The world works against faith and trust in God. Worldliness is the opposite of godliness. Here's what the Bible says about the world: "Do not love the world or anything in the world. If anyone loves the world, the love of the Father is not in him. For everything in the world—the cravings of sinful man, the lust of his eyes and the boasting of what he has and does—comes not from the Father but from the world. The world and its desires pass away, but the man who does the will of God lives forever" (1 John 2:15–17).

The Devil's Attack from the Inside

The devil uses the flesh (sinful nature) to attack you from the inside. He wants to coax you into becoming a traitor toward God.

> The flesh is the sinful part of our human nature.

The flesh is the sinful part of our human nature—we all have it, Christians too. The difference for a Christian is that we also have the Holy Spirit to help us.

Paul, a veteran Christian, expressed the believer's battle with his sinful flesh this way:

> I do not understand what I do. For what I want to do
> I do not do, but what I hate I do. . . . I know that nothing
> good lives in me, that is, in my sinful nature [flesh]. For I

have the desire to do what is good, but I cannot carry it out. For what I do is not the good I want to do; no, the evil I do not want to do—this I keep on doing. . . . So I find this law at work: When I want to do good, evil is right there with me. For in my inner being I delight in God's law; but I see another law at work in the members of my body, waging war against the law of my mind and making me a prisoner of the law of sin at work within my members. What a wretched man I am! Who will rescue me from this body of death? Thanks be to God—through Jesus Christ our Lord! (Romans 7:15–25).

The battle for your mind is a war that never ends. "When I want to do good, evil is right there with me." Until you are in heaven you will always be in a spiritual battle. One army is always defending the hill that the other army is trying to take back.

> *The battle for your mind is a war that never ends.*

But also notice God does not leave us mired in this muck. Jesus Christ will rescue us from this "body of death"—another term for our flesh.

Q *Pick one area in which you are repeatedly tempted. How well does Romans 7 capture what you're going through?*

Describe a day's worth of fighting for your mind. How many times would the hill be taken back and forth by the enemy?

On to Victory

I'm guessing that if you made it this far in the book, you are a young man who wants to do the right thing. Yet you no doubt sometimes find your thoughts conflicted, whipsawed, churning, surprise attacked, uncontrollable, doubting, moody, prideful, lustful, bizarre, heavily tempted, fantasizing, envious, jealous, and filled with anger—even rage.

How do you gain victory over your secret thought life? Since this is a spiritual problem, it requires a spiritual answer.

Having secret thoughts is a spiritual problem.

First, you must accept that there actually is a battle for your mind going on between your sinful nature (flesh) and God's Spirit. Galatians 5:17 says, "For the sinful nature [flesh] desires what is contrary to the Spirit, and the Spirit what is contrary to the sinful nature. They are in conflict with each other, so that you do not do what you want."

A lot of men "say" they believe this, but in their heart of hearts they really think it is up to them—they can handle temptation in their own strength. That would be a huge mistake for you.

Second, God never tempts anyone. Rather, it is our "own evil desires" (again, another term for flesh). "When tempted, no one should say, 'God is tempting me.' For God cannot be tempted by evil, nor does he tempt anyone; but each one is tempted when, by his own evil desire, he is dragged away and enticed. Then, after desire has conceived, it gives birth to sin; and sin, when it is full-grown, gives birth to death" (James 1:13–15).

Once you grasp the simplicity of this battle for your mind, you can equip yourself and fight back.

Once the simplicity of this battle is grasped, you can fight back.

God has not left you on your own. *God, Jesus, and the Holy Spirit* form the allied army. Jesus came not only to save us from our sins, but also to give us power to live holy, happy lives by faith. The Holy Spirit is here right now to give us victory over the world, the flesh, and the devil.

Q *Do you have any doubts that you are in a real spiritual battle, and why or why not?*
Where do evil desires come from?

Resisting Temptation

How to tell if you are losing the battle:

The acts of the sinful nature are obvious: sexual immorality, impurity and debauchery; idolatry and witchcraft; hatred, discord, jealousy, fits of rage, selfish ambition, dissensions, factions and envy; drunkenness, orgies, and the like. I warn you, as I did before, that those who live like this will not inherit the kingdom of God (Galatians 5:19–21).

How to tell if you are winning the battle:

But the fruit of the Spirit is love, joy, peace, patience, kindness, goodness, faithfulness, gentleness and self-control. Against such things there is no law. Those who belong to Christ Jesus have crucified the sinful nature with its passions and desires. Since we live by the Spirit, let us keep in step with the Spirit. Let us not become conceited, provoking and envying each other (Galatians 5:22–26).

Temptations are not sins. But every sin begins with a temptation—like losing your temper because you can't have your own way, a critical spirit, touchiness, or looking down on others. Temptations can be resisted.

If you depend on the power of the Holy Spirit, you will be able to resist the temptations of the flesh. "So I say, live by the Spirit, and you will not gratify the desires of the sinful nature" (Galatians 5:16).

Merely knowing that certain thoughts are sinful doesn't make them go away. We must exercise proactive faith. How do you do that? By depending upon the Holy Spirit.

How do you depend on the Holy Spirit? The Bible says God will faithfully give you the power (or strength) to resist temptation if you will turn to him in prayer and faith when tempted: "No temptation has seized you except what is common to man. And God is faithful; he will not let you be tempted beyond what you can bear. But when you are tempted, he will also provide a way out so that you can stand up under it" (1 Corinthians 10:13).

Q *How do you normally handle bad thoughts, and what would you do differently after reading this section? Have you been winning or losing the battle, and why?*

Forgiveness of Sins

There are no perfect people who always do right and never sin. In fact, every man sins daily. That's why we need an ongoing, authentic relationship with our Savior.

So, what can you do when you have blown it? Jesus is always and immediately available to forgive your sins and, by grace, give you a fresh start. "If we confess our sins, he is faithful and just and will forgive us our sins and purify us from all unrighteousness" (1 John 1:9).

Anytime you realize you have sinned, simply pause and confess it. By faith receive the forgiveness of Jesus. Thank him for being faithful and just. Surrender to his lordship and commit to follow him. This should be happening several times each day.

A Challenge

The seedbed for temptation and sin is the mind. Jesus said, "It is the thought-life that defiles you. For from within, out of a person's heart, come evil thoughts, sexual immorality, theft, murder, adultery, greed, wickedness, deceit, eagerness for lustful pleasure, envy, slander, pride, and foolishness. All these vile things come from within; they are what defile you and make you unacceptable to God" (Mark 7:20–23 NLT).

As you can see, the mind is the battleground—the hill the enemy is trying to take. You will never completely defeat the lusts of your flesh, the lures of the world, and the pride of life. They are soldiers in the devil's army, and they are always looking for a weak spot they can attack.

The key to ongoing victory is to guard your mind and heart through ongoing repentance and faith in Jesus. Watch what you read. Be careful about your friends. Consider the TV programs you watch. Choose your music wisely. Think about the messages in the movies you see.

But, please, don't get trapped into thinking that Christianity is about changing your behavior. It is about changing your mind—what you believe—and the changes in your behavior will follow naturally. This means getting at the root of your beliefs.

David Delk, a man I work with at Man in the Mirror, says, "Change the root and you will change the fruit." He talks about an orange tree in his backyard. He says, "If I decided I didn't want an orange tree anymore, I could go out and pick off every orange. Next I could go to the store, buy a bag full of apples and some tape, then come home and tape apples all over the tree.

"But what would happen next year? The oranges would be back. The only way to get rid of the oranges for good is to dig the tree up by the roots."

Changing your outward behavior will not change your life. To do that, you must change the way you believe. All sin, at the root, is the

THE YOUNG MAN IN THE MIRROR

result of unbelief. Willpower is no good until it flows out of a true surrender to the lordship of Jesus. That's the deal.

Q *Why won't mere willpower have any lasting effect on your
secret thoughts?*
*Are you prepared to surrender to the lordship of
Jesus, and why or why not?*

15 | suffering

In chapter 2, I said men want three main things:

1. *We want something we can give our lives to*—a cause or mission. Early in this book I called this, "I want to do something with my life."

2. *We want someone to share it with.* This is the need to love and be loved, to be part of a community, to find acceptance. We've spent some time on how a high school student can have healthy relationships.

3. *We want a "system" that offers a reasonable explanation for why 1 and 2 are so difficult.* This third "want" gets at the problem of suffering, which is the topic of this chapter.

The Problem of Suffering

James laughed along with all the guys when he sat in the banana cream pie that Brett slid under him as he sat down to eat his lunch.

But inside he felt humiliated and angry. He obviously didn't have a change of pants at school, so he had to walk around with soiled jeans for the rest of the day.

What he really wanted to do was punch out Brett's lights. What he really wanted to do was go crawl in a hole and feel sorry for himself. What he actually did was pretend it didn't hurt or bother him at all.

James couldn't help but wonder, *Why does there have to be so much pain to growing up?* He had suffered dozens of indignities. Twice—once in the sixth grade and once recently—he had been singled out in class for

129

not knowing an answer and felt put down. One day in sixth grade the class bully slugged him in the face and gave him a bloody nose. In the eighth grade he was turned down by a popular girl in front of everyone when he asked her to dance at a school function.

> *Put-downs, turndowns, bullied, irritated, sarcasm, loneliness, worry, rejection.*

As long as James could remember, his younger brother had purposely irritated him until he would lose his temper. When James finally couldn't take it any more, he would haul off and hit his brother, who would then run crying to his parents. It really bugged him that they would always punish him—the older brother—but let his younger brother go.

One of his teachers regularly made sarcastic remarks about students, and James was one of his regulars. His sixth grade teacher told him that he might want to consider a "vocational" high school because he didn't have what it takes for college. When James was ten his grandfather who had always taken him fishing died. It was an open-casket funeral. That image still flashed regularly into his mind.

For his twelfth birthday, his parents gave James a cocker spaniel puppy, which he named Cookie. He loved that dog so much. About a year later, Cookie was hit by a car. He didn't die right away, but it was obvious there was no way the dog could live. So his dad scooped Cookie into an empty cooler and took him to the vet to be put to sleep.

All these sufferings were in addition to the countless routine slights, rejections, phony friends, relationships that ended badly, sarcasms, colds, flus, headaches, pressures, and worries.

Until the ninth grade, James took all these sufferings in stride. He never questioned why the world could be such a harsh place. But over the years he met classmates who had suffered through much worse things than he had ever imagined.

One guy had been beaten several times by his alcoholic father. One of the girls he liked a lot got pregnant. She came from a broken home and she had never met her biological father. A couple of the guys in his group were depressed a lot because no matter how well they did, it never seemed to be enough to make their dads happy. A lot of his friends were in various stages of depression, largely because their parents didn't have enough time to listen to them. Some had parents who fought all the time. Several had parents who were divorced.

Many of the other kids were left on their own to raise themselves. Their parents were busy making money to buy things they didn't really want and never used anyway because they were always so busy.

The problem with suffering is that it really does hurt. Barbed comments from "friends" intended to embarrass you in front of girls. Being excluded from a party. A parent who's always on your case. Feelings of loneliness and isolation. Feeling like no one understands or cares.

There are sufferings like chronic physical pain, physical deformities, emotional pain, and the intangible pain of rejection. There are the more global sufferings of starving children overseas, major earthquakes that kill and dislodge thousands at a time, our own 9/11 terrorist attacks, famines, and grisly wars.

James realized that an *intangible* pain can afflict the soul and hurt far more than a *physical* pain that afflicts the body.

James and his family were pretty active in their church. James had learned about Noah, Moses, Joseph, David, and Christ from an early age. But it was not until he reached thirteen that he started to connect the dots between the "real world" in which he lived and the "ancient world" of the Bible.

He saw in the Bible that God's people had many troubles. He also saw that God did not always deliver people from their troubles right away, or easily. Yet, he did see that in the end God always took care of his people. But still he wondered . . .

Q *What are some ways you have suffered?*
How have you seen others suffer?
Are you suffering right now and, if so, how?

The Questions Raised by Suffering

> "If the universe is so bad, or even half so bad, how on earth did human beings ever come to attribute it to the activity of a wise and good creator?"

The world can be a brutal place. When Christian writer C. S. Lewis was an atheist, an odd thought struck him so hard that it put him on a path to becoming a Christian. He said, "There is one question which I never dreamed of raising. I never noticed that the very strength and facility of the pessimist's case at once poses us a problem. If the universe is so bad, or even half so bad, how on earth did human beings ever come to attribute it to the activity of a wise and good creator?"[15]

Part of your initiation into manhood is coming to terms with three great questions about God raised by suffering:

1. Does God know?
2. Does God care?
3. Can God do anything about it?

A God who doesn't know what we are going through would be *ignorant*. A God who doesn't care would be *malevolent*. A God who can't do anything about it would be *impotent*.

First, does God know? Often it just doesn't "feel" like God knows what we're going through. Does he?

If he doesn't, then he is not omniscient (all-knowing). But Christianity teaches that God is all-knowing. He knows our secret thought life, he knows our thoughts from afar, he knows every word we will speak before we say it (Psalm 139). He knows what you are going through.

Second, does God care? If God does know, then it doesn't "feel" like he cares. Does he care about our problems and pains?

If he doesn't, then he is not omni-benevolent (all-good). One of the core beliefs of Christian faith is the integrity of God—that he is an altogether good and righteous God who deeply loves and cares for those who love him and are called according to his purpose (Romans 8:28). He cares about what you are going through.

Third, can God do anything about it? If God does know and care, then often it doesn't "feel" like he has the power to do anything about it. Can God relieve our sufferings?

If he can't, then he is not omnipotent (all-powerful). A common prayer around the dinner table is, "God is great, God is good, and we thank him for this food. Amen."

No idea is more foundational in Christianity than the greatness, or omnipotence, of God.

- He made the earth by his power (Jeremiah 51:15).
- He rules forever by his power (Psalm 66:7).
- He rules over the nations (Psalm 22:28).
- By his power God raised Jesus from the dead, and he will raise us also (1 Corinthians 6:14).

What are your questions about suffering?

The Christian System

It would not be wise to seek out pain and suffering. But we don't have to. Pain and suffering will seek out us.

> Pain is a universal problem that every philosophy and religion must try to explain.

C. S. Lewis also noted, "Christianity is not a system into which we have to fit the awkward fact of pain; it is itself one of the awkward facts which have to be fitted into any system we make."

In other words, pain is a universal problem that every philosophy, system, story, worldview, and religion must try to explain.

Lewis went on to say, "In a sense, (Christianity) creates, rather than solves, the problem of pain, for pain would be no problem unless, side by side with our daily experience of this painful world, we have received what we think a good assurance that ultimate reality (God) is righteous and loving."[16]

One of the most satisfying elements of Christian faith is how beautifully it explains the questions raised by human suffering.

In chapter 3, I mentioned a business saying, "Your system is perfectly designed to produce the result you are getting." Christianity is a system perfectly designed to answer the questions raised by suffering.

God has a system perfectly designed to produce the results he wants. He is building us each into what the Bible calls a "new creation" (2 Corinthians 5:17). Through each of our sufferings, God adds to our faith, humility, holiness, obedience, wisdom, reverence, and worship.

> Your system is perfectly designed to produce the result you are getting.

Suffering is part of the calculus of Christianity—and every other system, or story. Remember what men want? We want something to live for, someone to share it with, and a "system" that gives a reasonable explanation why the first two wants are so difficult. The New Living Translation Bible offers an extensive explanation for suffering:

- "Dear friends, don't be surprised at the fiery trials you are going through, as if something strange were happening to you" (1 Peter 4:12).

- "For you have been given not only the privilege of trusting in Christ but also the privilege of suffering for him" (Philippians 1:29).

- "They encouraged them to continue in the faith, reminding them that they must enter into the Kingdom of God through many tribulations" (Acts 14:22).

- "Yes, and everyone who wants to live a godly life in Christ Jesus will suffer persecution" (2 Timothy 3:12).

- "My child, don't ignore it when the Lord disciplines you, and don't be discouraged when he corrects you. For the Lord disciplines those he loves, and he punishes those he accepts as his children" (Hebrews 12:5–6).

> *Don't be surprised. Suffering for Christ is a privilege. We enter heaven through many tribulations.*

All we want is satisfied in the gospel of Jesus. He is the cause, he is the someone, he is the "system" that explains the meaning and purpose of life. This system explains suffering without explaining it away. The gospel of Jesus offers a satisfying and redemptive explanation for why life is so messy.

All systems have to tackle the problem of suffering. In Christianity, God uses suffering for good, without ceasing to call it suffering. Through sufferings we have fellowship with Jesus (Philippians 3:10).

President George W. Bush said, "The promise of faith is not the absence of suffering; it is the presence of grace."

We tap into the Christian system and God's power to deliver us through prayer and faith in the grace of Jesus.

Q *Are you satisfied that Christianity is a system that answers the problems raised by suffering, even if you don't understand all the specifics? If not, what still troubles you?*

The Purpose of Suffering

We have been made in a way that we can handle almost anything if we believe it has a purpose. During WWII the Nazis forced prisoners to make bombs to use against their own people. One day the hated factory was bombed.

> There is comfort in suffering because there is purpose to suffering.

The commandant formed the prisoners at one end of the yard. He made them fill wheelbarrows full of the ruins, then cart them to the other end of the prison yard and empty them. Then, he made them fill the wheelbarrows again with the same materials, cart them back to where they started, and empty them. Back and forth, over and over again.

Soon, the prisoners began to go crazy. One ran away and was shot. Another ran into the electrified fence and was killed. The prisoners had been able to handle tremendous persecution—making bombs for their enemies—when they at least saw some purpose in what they did. But the senseless act of carting rubble from one end of the prison yard to the other was too much.[17]

For the Christian, there is comfort in suffering because there is purpose to suffering. God is making us like his Son, Jesus.

Q *Describe a time of suffering that resulted in good. How is it comforting to know that God makes all things work together for good when we love him and are called according to his purpose?*

A Challenge

My daughter had graduated from college and taken a job. Early one Monday morning we were talking on the phone. She said, "Well, how are you doing, Dad?"

> *Sometimes we will experience delirious joy. . . .*

I said, "Jen, I am experiencing delirious joy." Delirious joy is something that I experience almost every day. Usually it revolves around my private devotions with the Lord in the morning. Of course, after I get absorbed in my daily work, the delirious part fades away.

She said, "Dad, I think that is wonderful. But for me, though, I find that I need to practice deliberate joy." What an insightful distinction.

Most of us will live an "80–20" life. I mean that something like 80 percent of our lives will be pretty normal and happy, but about 20 percent of our lives will be associated with trials, temptations, pains, bad things, letdowns, discouragements—in a word: suffering.

No matter what our circumstances, we can always practice deliberate joy. In fact, we are commanded to do so: "Rejoice always" (1 Thessalonians 5:16–18 HCSB). It is not supposed to be optional. We can do this by accepting the challenge to be a deliberately joyful man.

Even in the 80 percent of our times that are normal and happy, we will only experience delirious joy occasionally. Most of the time, even when things go well, we will need to practice deliberate joy.

Q *What percent of the time are you joyful?*

> *When bad things happen to you, are you still able to be joyful, and why or why not?*

> *What remaining questions do you have about suffering?*

> *Most of the time, however, we will need to practice deliberate joy.*

afterword

Congratulations. You have been "asked up" into manhood. You have responded by reading this book as a rite of passage—an initiation into manhood.

How you choose to handle the issues we've explored will impact you for the rest of your life. Choose wisely.

In the introduction I said, "You are going to be a man. The question is, will you be a good one or a bad one?"

According to the Bible, manhood is a new way of talking, thinking, and reasoning: "When I was a child, I talked like a child, I thought like a child, I reasoned like a child. When I became a man, I put childish ways behind me" (1 Corinthians 13:11).

God is looking for men who want to share their lives with Christ by loving and serving him with all their hearts.

God is looking for men who want to model to the world a system perfectly designed to produce abundant life now—though not without troubles—and eternal life in the world to come.

"He who began a good work in you will carry it on to completion until the day of Christ Jesus" (Philippians 1:6). So don't be afraid.

Glorify God with your life. Enjoy him—he certainly enjoys you.

discussion leader's guide

Any father, youth worker, or mentor can lead a Young Man in the Mirror *discussion group. You don't have to be an experienced Bible teacher to lead a discussion.*

Suggestions for a Discussion Leader

Getting Started

- Photocopy the table of contents. Give to young men you want to meet with. Ask them if they would like to be in a group that would read the book and answer discussion questions in each chapter.
- The optimum size is four to six young men; seven is max.
- Plan to cover one chapter a week for fifteen weeks (this will no doubt take longer because of other scheduled events and holidays). You could also consider doing two chapters per week and meet for 8 sessions.

First Week

- Distribute a copy of the book to each young man.
- Have each young man introduce himself and answer an icebreaker question like, "Why are you interested in this study group?"
- Jump right in and read the first chapter together and answer the questions.

Proposed Meeting Schedule

- Plan to meet for 1 1/2 hours weekly.
- Thirty minutes—pizza, wings, or Chinese food with soft drinks. Consider varying the menu.
- Sixty minutes—read and discuss one chapter, a section at a time. Close in prayer.

Reading the Book and Leading the Discussion

- Not all the young men will be able to read the chapters in advance, so forget that idea unless you have some special powers! (or a very unusual group). Instead, read the book out loud one section at a time. Use a different young man to read each section.

- Answer the question(s) at the end of each section identified by this symbol: **Q**. The questions will always look like this:

Q *"You are not abnormal." Do you agree or not, and why? How does it make you feel to know that you are not abnormal?*

- If a young man asks you a question beyond your scope, simply say so and move on.

How to Have Great Meetings

- Call your young men each week to remind them of the meeting.
- Read the chapter yourself in advance.
- Look up and read Bible verses that support points being made.
- Lead your young men into a meaningful discussion based upon the questions at the end of sections.
- Make sure every young man gets "air time."
- Share from your own experience.
- Be vulnerable.
- Answer the secret questions the young men are too embarrassed to ask.
- Deal in their reality, not yours.
- Start and end on time.
- Include prayer to start and end—have the young men pray if it seems right to you.

Things to Avoid

- Don't preach or teach. Rather, lead a discussion by asking the questions at the end of each section and by offering nondogmatic advice when appropriate.
- Don't speak more than 25 percent of the time.
- Don't go off on tangents. Stick to the topic of the day.

- Don't feel pressure to fill in the "quiet" after you ask a question. Let one of your young men break the silence.
- Don't ever put anyone down.
- Don't be sarcastic.
- Don't spiritualize when a practical answer is what they really want.

Graduation Ceremonies

- Plan a graduation ceremony, picnic, father/mentor and son retreat, or other event with fathers and mentors.
- Purchase blank certificates at an office supply store, put in "initiation into manhood" text, you and each father or mentor sign, and present at your graduation ceremony.
  (See sample certificate on the next page.)
- Father/Mentor and Son Cookout. Have an activity that will appeal to your young men (my group did jet skis on our lake). Gather everyone in a circle after burgers or BBQ. Have each father or mentor write out a two-minute blessing in advance on "Why I love you and why I am proud of you." Have each father/mentor share first. Then, as the leader, pick one word that describes each young man and offer a tribute. Present each young man with his certificate signed by you and the father/mentor.
- Church Ceremony. Use as much imagination as you want. For example, you could have the young men stand before the church (possibly with their father/mentor at their side) and have the elders or deacons gather around, have the pastor acknowledge what they have completed, then offer a prayer of initiation into manhood.
- Consider videotaping your event and giving each young man a copy.
- Have someone act as the official photographer to get candids and a group photo. Give a 5 x 7 of the group photo to each young man.

THIS CERTIFICATE
IS PRESENTED TO

_____

for successfully completing

THE YOUNG MAN IN THE MIRROR STUDY GROUP

as part of your initiation into manhood

May you experience the love and grace of Jesus Christ in all that you think, say, and do.

_____   _____

Discussion Leader   *Father/Mentor*

notes

1. Neil Postman, "Learning by Story," *The Atlantic Monthly*, December 1989, 122–24.

2. Adapted from Postman, "Learning by Story," and Mardi Keyes, *Who Invented Adolescence?* (Rochester: Ransom Fellowship, 1994).

3. C. S. Lewis, *God in the Dock* (Grand Rapids: Wm. B. Eerdmans, 1970), 280. Lewis said you can't get second things by putting them first. Every preference of a small good to a great, or a partial good to a total good, involves the loss of the small or partial good for which the sacrifice was made.

4. From Frederick Taylor, the father of Scientific Management.

5. J. Gresham Machen, *Christianity and Liberalism* (Grand Rapids: Wm. B. Eerdmans Publishing Co., 1923), 48.

6. G. K. Chesterton, *Orthodoxy* (New York: Doubleday, 1908, 1990), 132.

7. Mardi Keyes, *Who Invented Adolescence?* (Rochester: Ransom Fellowship, 1994), 12.

8. Ibid., 84.

9. All truth is God's truth. Gardner's theory of multiple intelligences has the ring of truth. No doubt his theory will be improved in the years ahead but, in the meantime, it makes a meaningful contribution to understanding how God has made us.

10. Howard Gardner, *Frames of Mind: The Theory of Multiple Intelligences* (New York: Basic Books, 1983, 1993).

11. These, along with the definitions of speaking and signifying gifts that follow, are adapted from the work of Carl Smith, Kenneth O. Gangel, and Leslie B. Flynn.

12. This section is adapted from my book *Discipleship and the Man in the Mirror,* chapter 15: "Seven Ways to Find God's Will" (Grand Rapids: Zondervan, 1992).

13. James Dobson, *Bringing Up Boys* (Wheaton: Tyndale House, 2001), 127.

14. C. S. Lewis, *Mere Christianity* (New York: Macmillan, 1943), 108–9.

15. C. S. Lewis, *The Problem of Pain* (New York: Macmillan, 1962), 15.

16. Ibid., 24.

17. Charles Colson and Ellen Santilli Vaughn, *Kingdoms in Conflict* (Grand Rapids: Zondervan Publishing House, 1987), 67–68.

about the author

Business leader, author, and speaker, Patrick Morley has been used throughout the world to help men and leaders think more deeply about their lives and to equip them to have a larger impact on the world.

He founded Morley Properties, which, during the 1980s, was one of Florida's one hundred largest privately held companies. He has been the president or managing partner of fifty-nine companies and partnerships.

Mr. Morley graduated with honors from the University of Central Florida, which selected him to receive its Distinguished Alumnus Award in 1984. He successfully completed the Harvard Graduate School of Business Owner/President Management Program and is a graduate of Reformed Theological Seminary.

He is author of *The Man in the Mirror,* which has sold over two million copies, along with many other books.

Patrick Morley has served as president or chairman of numerous civic and professional organizations. He founded the Thanksgiving Leadership Prayer Breakfast in Orlando and, since its inception in 1978, has served as its chairman. Patrick is a cofounder and chairman of the National Coalition for Men's Ministry and also serves on the editorial board of *New Man Magazine.* Every Friday he teaches a Bible study called TGIF for 150 businessmen and leaders.

One of the pioneers in the Christian Men's Movement, he founded the ministry in 1992 called Man in the Mirror, for which he serves as president and chairman. The desire of Man in the Mirror is to partner with churches to reach men in America with a compelling opportunity to be transformed by Jesus Christ.

Patrick Morley lives with his family in Orlando, Florida.